TEACHER GUIDE FOR

Surviving the City

Volumes 1–3: Exploring Identity, Allyship, and Social Action for Meaningful Change in Grades 7–12

Created by Christine M'Lot

I0805586

Portage & Main Press gratefully acknowledges the financial support of the Government of Canada as well as the Province of Manitoba through the Department of Sport, Culture, Heritage and Tourism and the Manitoba Book Publishing Tax Credit for our publishing activities.

Funded by the Government of Canada
Financé par le gouvernement du Canada | Canada

Printed and bound in Canada by Rapido Books
Design by Jennifer Lum
Cover Art by Natasha Donovan

Thank you to Tasha Spillett for creating a beautiful work of literature in which students can see reflections of themselves, their families, and their communities.
—*CM*

ISBN 978-1-77492-140-1
Also issued in electronic format: ISBN 978-1-77492-141-8 (PDF)

28 27 26 25 1 2 3 4 5

PORTAGE & MAIN PRESS
www.portageandmainpress.com
Winnipeg, Manitoba
Treaty 1 Territory and homeland of the Métis Nation

CONTENTS

USING THIS GUIDE

THIS TEACHER GUIDE is meant to be a no-prep resource for educators to use either for individual stand-alone lessons or as a complete unit plan. Throughout the lessons presented in this teacher guide, students will be learning about, exploring, researching, and presenting on essential themes that arise in the graphic novel. Students will conduct inquiry into a social issue of their choosing for the Social-Justice Action Project in lesson 6. For grades 7–8 this lesson may be a class project or an individual project, while we suggest older students work in groups of three to five.

The Surviving the City series is made up of three volumes. Volume 1 is titled *Surviving the City*, volume 2 *From the Roots Up*, and volume 3 *We Are the Medicine*. In this guide, when referring to the entire series we will call it the Surviving the City series. When referring to a particular volume, we will use its individual title. The lesson plan for lesson 1 assumes that students have already read the first two volumes; the remaining lesson plans assume students have already read the series in its entirety.

This teacher guide is best suited for use in classes such as Grades 7–12 English, Grade 12 Global Issues, and Grade 11 and 12 Current Topics in First Nations, Métis, and Inuit Studies. The lesson plans are formatted using the Activate, Acquire, Apply, and Assess (AAAA) format for ease of use. Activate activities are used to invoke prior knowledge on a topic or to introduce themes in the lesson. Acquire activities will include lessons on various topics relating to the graphic novel. Apply activities give the students the opportunity to demonstrate learning, while Assess activities have students complete an assignment to demonstrate the appropriate learning outcomes. Rubrics are included in this guide, with an emphasis on co-constructing pieces of each rubric with students.

Many activities throughout the lessons incorporate Indigenous pedagogical practice by having students work collaboratively. Other activities have students take on the role of expert and teacher, and these lessons often involve student-led research. Working in relation with others, seeking holism in understanding, and learning through storytelling are key practices in Indigenous pedagogy. This teacher guide aims to serve as a tool for engaging students in the complexity of understanding and embracing worldviews that may be different from their own. Other helpful resources related to Indigenous pedagogy include:

- *Achieving Indigenous Student Success: A Guide for Secondary Classrooms* by Pamela Rose Toulouse
- *Ensouling Our Schools: A Universally Designed Framework for Mental Health, Well-Being, and Reconciliation* by Jennifer Katz with Kevin Lamoureux
- Indspire: <https://indspire.ca/programs/educators/>
- Manitoba First Nations Education Resource Centre: <https://mfnerc.org/>
- *Potlatch as Pedagogy: Learning Through Ceremony* by Sara Florence Davidson and Robert Davidson
- *Resurgence: Engaging With Indigenous Narratives and Cultural Expressions In and Beyond the Classroom* by Christine M'Lot and Katya Adamov Ferguson
- *Truth and Reconciliation in Canadian Schools* by Pamela Rose Toulouse
- *Wayi Wah! Indigenous Pedagogies: An Act for Reconciliation and Anti-Racist Education* by Jo Chrona

CONSIDERATIONS FOR TEACHING GRAPHIC NOVELS

The term *comics* refers to an artistic medium that combines verbal and visual information in a sequential order, often to tell a story. The term *graphic novel* describes a specific book format for comics, rather than a genre. Graphic novels and comic books can be fiction, nonfiction, biography, fantasy, dystopia, or any genre in between.[1] Graphic novels are an accessible reading resource for all students, and they have been proven to engage even the most reluctant of readers.[2] Graphic novels also include dialogue, characters' thoughts, narration, and captions. Graphic novels are typically read from left to right, and top to bottom.

The first lesson in this guide is designed to introduce teachers and students alike to the comics medium and the graphic novel form. For more information and ideas for using graphic novels in the classroom, see the resource *Teaching With Graphic Novels* by Shelley Stagg Peterson, available through Portage & Main Press.

---

1 "What is a Graphic Novel?" Get Graphic, the Buffalo and Erie County Public Library and Partnering Organizations, accessed August 1, 2019, https://www.buffalolib.org/get-graphic/what-graphic-novel.

2 Sarah Knutson, "How Graphic Novels Help Students Develop Critical Skills," Resilient Educator, updated October 23, 2018, https://resilienteducator.com/classroom-resources/graphic-novels-visual-literacy/.

CO-CONSTRUCTING CRITERIA

The rubrics in this guide are designed to be co-constructed with students. Co-constructing criteria with students is an effective way to support students in becoming self-directed, independent learners who are also critical thinkers. Partially completed rubric templates are included in this guide so students can co-construct the missing pieces. Students are tasked with determining the most important pieces of the lesson, along with what a successful product will look like. They can accomplish this based on examining what is already present and thinking about what other criteria would classify an assignment as developing (needing improvement), good, or excellent. We encourage teachers to either co-construct the criteria as a whole class or organize students into small groups to create their own assessment criteria that can be shared during class discussions. If available, we encourage teachers to show students examples of previous student work. After viewing sample work, students can discuss what made the work effective and what could be improved. This discussion can guide students in creating their own assessment criteria.

The following resource from the Saskatchewan School Library Association may be helpful for co-constructing criteria: "Using Samples to Co-Construct Criteria for Writing," available at <https://www.learnsask.net/uploads/9/5/3/6/95368874/11_usingcriteria_to_co-constructcriteriaforwriting_schampmvaughn_winter2011.pdf>.

INDIGENOUS PERSPECTIVES AND HISTORY

Indigenous perspectives are now part of the curriculum in every province in Canada. Further, the National Truth and Reconciliation Commission's Calls to Action #62 and #63 deal directly with Indigenous education, stating:

> 62. We call upon the federal, provincial, and territorial governments, in consultation and collaboration with Survivors, Aboriginal peoples, and educators, to:
>
> i. Make age-appropriate curriculum on residential schools, Treaties, and Aboriginal peoples' historical and contemporary contributions to Canada a mandatory education requirement for Kindergarten to Grade Twelve students.
>
> ii. Provide the necessary funding to post-secondary institutions to educate teachers on how to integrate Indigenous knowledge and teaching methods into classrooms.
>
> iii. Provide the necessary funding to Aboriginal schools to utilize Indigenous knowledge and teaching methods in classrooms.

iv. Establish senior-level positions in government at the assistant deputy minister level or higher dedicated to Aboriginal content in education.

63. We call upon the Council of Ministers of Education, Canada to maintain an annual commitment to Aboriginal education issues, including:

i. Developing and implementing Kindergarten to Grade Twelve curriculum and learning resources on Aboriginal peoples in Canadian history, and the history and legacy of residential schools.

ii. Sharing information and best practices on teaching curriculum related to residential schools and Aboriginal history.

iii. Building student capacity for intercultural understanding, empathy, and mutual respect.

iv. Identifying teacher-training needs relating to the above.[3]

Aspects of Indigenous pedagogy are woven throughout this teacher guide to enhance students' understanding of Indigenous worldviews. Circle pedagogy is used throughout this resource as a way to show the interconnectedness of ideas and topics. Students will have the opportunity to select, research, and present on an Indigenous resistance movement.

According to Manitoba Education and Youth's *Integrating Aboriginal Perspectives Into Curricula* document (2003), implementing Indigenous perspectives has a number of positive effects in the classroom, including:

- helping Indigenous students develop a positive self-identity through learning their own histories, cultures, traditional values, contemporary lifestyles, and traditional knowledge
- helping Indigenous students to participate in a learning environment that will equip them with the knowledge and skills needed to participate more fully in the unique civic and cultural realities of their communities
- helping non-Indigenous students develop an understanding and respect for the histories, traditional values, contemporary lifestyles, and traditional knowledge of Indigenous Peoples
- helping non-Indigenous students develop informed opinions on matters relating to Indigenous Peoples[4]

3 Truth and Reconciliation Commission of Canada, *Truth and Reconciliation Commission of Canada: Calls to Action* (2015), 7.

4 Manitoba Education and Youth, *Integrating Aboriginal Perspectives Into Curricula: A Resource for Curriculum Developers, Teachers, and Administrators* (2003).

CONSIDERATIONS FOR TEACHING THE SURVIVING THE CITY SERIES

Sensitive themes are likely to come up when reading the Surviving the City series and learning about Indigenous topics. This graphic novel series deals with sensitive topics such as racism, caregiver illness, the child welfare system, residential schools, Missing and Murdered Indigenous Women and Girls and Two-Spirit People, the unmarked graves of children at residential schools, and police brutality. Both teacher and student mental health should be prioritized during this time. It is important that you inform your students about resources that are available to them if they should feel overwhelmed or upset by the content at any point throughout the readings. Teachers should also know which resources are available to them through their school divisions, teacher's society, or community. Teachers should create a safe and open learning environment where students' mental health is supported. Often, having direct discussions about mental health and wellness is a great way for your students to hear from others and learn positive coping skills to help you all through this learning journey. Lesson 5: What Is Wellness From a Holistic Perspective? touches on the subject of wellness through a holistic lens.

Two-Spirit

Many Indigenous communities around the continent are known to have recognized more than two genders prior to colonization, as Albert McLeod explains in "What Does Two-Spirit Mean?" which you will find on page 64 of *From the Roots Up*, volume 2 of the Surviving the City series. In fact, many Indigenous languages have words to describe people who do not fit the gender binary of either man or woman. For example, the Navajo refer to a Two-Spirit individual as *Nádleehí* (one who is transformed). The Lakota refer to *Winkté*, which is indicative of a man who behaves as a woman. *Niizh Manidoowag* means *Two-Spirit* in Anishinaabemowin, and *Hemaneh* means *half man, half woman* in Cheyenne.[5] Sadly, during the residential school era, generations of Indigenous children were taught that anyone outside of the gender binary of male and female—or any practice outside the norms of heterosexual sex—was bad, shameful, and wrong.

Today, *Two-Spirit* is a term some Indigenous 2SLGBTQ+ people use to describe their spiritual identity as having both a male and female spirit. The term can also be used to describe gender identity (male, female, third gender) and/or sexual identity (lesbian, gay, bisexual, queer). Elder Myra Laramee is credited with coining the term at the third annual international LGBT Native American gathering held in Winnipeg in 1990.[6] Many Indigenous communities and individuals around the continent are working to restore Two-Spirit teachings and roles in community.

---

5 Duane Brayboy, "Two Spirits, One Heart, Five Genders," *Indian Country Today*, accessed March 9, 2024, https://ictnews.org/archive/two-spirits-one-heart-five-genders.

6 "About Us: Our History," Two-Spirit Manitoba, accessed March 23, 2024, https://twospiritmanitoba.ca/about-us.

  ISBN: 978-1-77492-140-1

Intersectionality

One of the main themes in the Surviving the City series is *intersectionality*. *Intersectionality* refers to the layered marginalization people may experience when they belong to more than one marginalized group in society. The term was coined in 1989 by Black legal scholar Kimberlé Crenshaw, who wrote "Demarginalizing the Intersection of Race and Sex: A Black Feminist Critique of Antidiscrimination Doctrine, Feminist Theory and Antiracist Politics." In this essay Crenshaw argues that the "marginalization and discrimination experienced by a Black woman cannot be understood in terms of racism or of sexism considered independently but must include the interactions."[7] Her groundbreaking essay opened the doors for people to begin speaking about and understanding how various aspects of their identities intersect to create layered experiences of oppression and power.

In *Surviving the City*, readers are exposed to characters who must navigate the various intersections of their identities. Readers will learn about Miikwaan and Dez's identities as Indigenous youth growing up in the city. They will see how both race and age affect these characters. In *From the Roots Up*, readers learn more about Dez's self-understanding as both an Indigenous and Two-Spirit youth. Readers will also see how race, age, gender, and sexuality intersect for Dez. In *We Are the Medicine*, readers are introduced to Ginebig, an Afro-Indigenous character. Through Ginebig readers will see how Indigenous and African identities intersect. Through the series' varied cast of characters, readers will observe and discuss how different identities interact with each other and ways that multiple identities can impact us.

Afro-Indigeneity

The term Afro-Indigenous is used to describe people who have both Indigenous and African lineages. In the article "Hair and the Ties That Bind," author Tasha Spillett explores her biracial and gender identity as a Black, Indigenous woman. The article will be assigned for students to read in lesson 2.

WHAT IS TRAUMA-INFORMED PRACTICE?

Trauma-informed practice means consciously working "to understand how violence, victimization, and other traumatic experiences" affect individuals. It also includes extending this understanding "to the provision of services and the design of systems so that they accommodate the needs and vulnerabilities of trauma survivors."[8] Although originally designed as a framework for delivering social services, trauma-informed practice is relevant to educational settings when students are learning about topics that could traumatize (or retraumatize) them. The goal of trauma-informed practice is to decrease the likelihood of traumatizing students

7 "Intersectionality," *Anti-Oppression*, Simmons University Library, accessed March 9, 2024, https://simmons.libguides.com/anti-oppression.

8 Lisa D. Butler, Filomena M. Critelli, and Elaine S. Rinfrette, "Trauma-Informed Care and Mental Health," *Directions in Psychiatry* 31, no. 3 (January 2011): 197–208, https://www.researchgate.net/publication/234155324_Trauma-Informed_Care_and_Mental_Health.

  ISBN: 978-1-77492-140-1

through exposing them to traumatic narratives. For example, the discussion of the unmarked graves being found at former residential schools in *We Are the Medicine* can be (re)traumatizing to students, so teachers are encouraged to give students advance warning of the subject matter, ensure they know which mental health resources are available to them, and allow students to debrief how they are feeling at the end of the lesson.

TEACHING DIFFICULT TOPICS FROM A TRAUMA-INFORMED STANCE

As is often true when learning about Indigenous subjects, sensitive topics may come up when your students are reading, researching, or learning about the Surviving the City series. The stories told through these graphic novels describe traumatic experiences such as racism, caregiver illness, the child welfare system, residential schools, Missing and Murdered Indigenous Women and Girls and Two-Spirit People, the unmarked graves of children at residential schools, and police brutality.

It is very likely that a student in your class has experienced being part of the child welfare system, so the themes in the Surviving the City series may be especially emotional for them to learn about. A trauma-informed practice uses the utmost caution and care while teaching about difficult topics. For example, informing the students in advance about which difficult topics will be covered on what day, passing around a resource sheet before you begin the lesson, reviewing coping mechanisms as a class for reading or viewing scenes that may be traumatizing, and giving students the option to sit out and do an alternative reading or activity if they wish are ways that we can support students' mental health.

Teaching about difficult topics from a trauma-informed stance means placing a high emphasis on informing students about resources that are available to them if they should feel overwhelmed or upset at any point. Throughout the process of preparing to read, reading, and responding to this story, create a safe and open learning environment where students' mental health is supported. For example, direct discussions about mental health and wellness are great ways for students to hear from others and learn positive coping skills to help them in their learning journeys.

Helpful information and advice for teachers on how to build flourishing learning communities and address mental health needs with all students can be found in *Ensouling Our Schools: A Universally Designed Framework for Mental Health, Well-Being, and Reconciliation* by Jennifer Katz with Kevin Lamoureux. Further, advice for teachers on how to take care of themselves can be found in *Teacher, Take Care* by Jennifer E. Lawson. For a list of more mental health resources, please see the Canadian Mental Health Association (CMHA) website. Here, you can find information about mental health services in your region, or check in on your mental health by completing the Mental Health Meter, What's Your Stress Index? test, or the Work-Life Balance Quiz. Visit the website at <https://cmha.ca>.

Finally, while reading this graphic novel with your class, include positive aspects of Indigenous histories and cultures to show the beauty and resilience in Indigenous communities. Suggested in this resource are ways to bring Indigenous cultures, languages, traditions, and

  ISBN: 978-1-77492-140-1

beliefs into your classroom; these include inviting an Elder or Knowledge Keeper to speak to your students about the various positive aspects of Indigenous cultures. Keep in mind that Indigenous Nations are distinct and each have their own cultures, languages, ceremonies, stories, and traditions. Learning about the positive aspects of Indigenous cultures can be a strong protective factor for Indigenous students who are learning about difficult topics.

INVITING AN ELDER INTO YOUR LEARNING SPACE

Teachers may want to engage the larger community and invite an Elder or Knowledge Keeper into their classroom to share stories, knowledge, or teachings with the class. Manitoba Education and Youth defines an Elder as "any person regarded or chosen by an Aboriginal nation to be the keeper and teacher of its oral tradition and knowledge," but it is important to remember that this definition may vary from community to community.[9] Here are some guidelines on building a positive relationship with a local Elder or Knowledge Keeper.

Preparing to Meet With an Elder

- Ask your local school board if they have an Elder-in-residence or a trusted Elder or Knowledge Keeper that they often ask to speak with students. You should always try to invite a local Elder first.
- Research the local protocols for inviting an Elder to speak with your class. Often, this will involve the passing of tobacco.
- Arrange a meeting between yourself and the Elder well in advance of the visit to your class.

Meeting With an Elder

- Share a bit about yourself and your family's history.
- Listen to and learn from the Elder.
- Adhere to the protocols in your area, and ask the Elder if they would be interested in sharing their gifts with your class.
- Be as flexible about the day and time for the visit as you can. Decide this together!
- Ask if the Elder needs any special accommodations for when they come.
- Discuss fair compensation. The Elder may be taking the day off work to accommodate your needs, so it is essential that they are well compensated for their time, energy, and emotional labour.
- Ask the Elder how they would like to be introduced to your class, and respect their preferences.

9 Manitoba Education and Youth, *Integrating Aboriginal Perspectives into Curricula: A Resource for Curriculum Developers, Teachers, and Administrators* (2003).

Preparing Your Students for an Elder's Visit

- Inform students that an Elder will be visiting the class. Ask if anyone knows what an Elder is, and discuss the important roles they have in our communities. Share that Elders are people who hold sacred teachings and should be treated with the utmost respect.
- Share with students why you decided to invite an Elder into the classroom.
- Ask if any students would like to volunteer to give the Elder a tobacco tie (or other gift, depending on the protocol of your region). Brief students about the protocol, and why it is important to thank the Elder in this way.

Day of the Visit to Your Class

- Welcome the Elder to your class/school. Have a student present the Elder with the tobacco tie (or other gift, depending on the protocol in your region).
- Give the Elder a tour of your school, if possible, or at least make sure they know where the washrooms are.
- Ensure that students are respectful while the Elder is speaking.
- Thank the Elder at the end and present them with the honorarium.

Try to build a relationship with a local Elder or Knowledge Keeper. Relationships take time to develop, so you should contact the Elder as soon as possible. If the day goes well, make sure to let them know that you will be inviting them back again. You could also have students write a thank-you card to the Elder as a way of showing appreciation.

CURRICULUM CONNECTIONS

BRITISH COLUMBIA: ENGLISH LANGUAGE ARTS 7, 8, 9

Curricular Competencies[10] Using oral, written, visual, and digital texts, students are expected individually and collaboratively to be able to:	Lesson					
	1	2	3	4	5	6
Apply appropriate strategies to comprehend written, oral, and visual texts, guide inquiry, and extend thinking	X	X	X	X		X
Recognize and appreciate how different features, forms, and genres of texts reflect different purposes, audiences, and messages	X	X	X	X		X
Think critically, creatively, and reflectively to explore ideas within, between, and beyond texts	X	X	X	X		X
Recognize and identify the role of personal, social, and cultural contexts, values, and perspectives in texts	X	X	X	X		X
Recognize how language constructs personal, social, and cultural identity	X	X	X	X		
Construct meaningful personal connections between self, text, and world	X	X	X	X	X	X
Understand how literary elements, techniques, and devices enhance and shape meaning	X	X	X	X		X
Recognize and appreciate the role of story, narrative, and oral tradition in expressing First Peoples perspectives, values, beliefs, and points of view	X	X		X		
Exchange ideas and viewpoints to build shared understanding and extend thinking	X	X	X	X	X	X
Use writing and design processes to plan, develop, and create engaging and meaningful literary and informational texts for a variety of purposes and audiences	X	X	X	X		X
Select and use appropriate features, forms, and genres according to audience, purpose, and message	X	X	X	X		

10 Based on *BC's Curriculum: English Language Arts*. https://curriculum.gov.bc.ca/curriculum/english-language-arts

BRITISH COLUMBIA: ENGLISH FIRST PEOPLES LITERARY STUDIES 10

Curricular Competencies [11] Using oral, written, visual, and digital texts, students are expected individually and collaboratively to be able to:	**Lesson**					
	1	**2**	**3**	**4**	**5**	**6**
Recognize and appreciate the role of story, narrative, and oral tradition in expressing First Peoples perspectives, values, beliefs, and points of view		X	X	X	X	X
Recognize and appreciate the diversity within and across First Peoples societies as represented in texts		X	X	X	X	X
Apply appropriate strategies in a variety of contexts to guide inquiry, extend thinking, and comprehend texts		X	X	X		X
Construct meaningful personal connections between self, text, and world	X	X	X	X	X	X
Think critically, creatively, and reflectively to explore ideas within, between, and beyond texts	X	X	X	X	X	X
Recognize and appreciate how different forms, structures, and features of texts reflect diverse purposes, audiences, and messages	X	X		X		X
Recognize the impact of personal, social, and cultural identities in First Peoples texts		X	X	X	X	X
Examine how literary elements, techniques, and devices enhance and shape meaning and impact	X	X		X		X
Assess the authenticity of First Peoples texts		X		X		
Identify bias, contradictions, and distortions				X		
Respectfully exchange ideas and viewpoints from diverse perspectives to build shared understandings and extend thinking		X	X	X		X
Respond to text in personal, creative, and critical ways	X	X	X	X	X	X
Demonstrate speaking and listening skills in a variety of formal and informal contexts for a range of purposes		X	X	X		X
Recognize intellectual property rights and community protocols and apply them as necessary				X		
Use the conventions of First Peoples and other Canadian spelling, syntax, and diction proficiently and as appropriate to the context	X	X	X	X		X

11 Based on *BC's Curriculum: English Literary Studies 10*. https://curriculum.gov.bc.ca/curriculum/english-language-arts/10/efp-literary-studies

Express an opinion and support it with evidence		X		X		X
Assess and refine texts to improve clarity and impact	X	X	X	X		X
Content Students are expected to know the following:						
Text forms and genres	X					
Common themes in First Peoples texts		X	X	X		
Reconciliation in Canada			X	X		X
First Peoples oral traditions • purposes of First Peoples oral text				X		
Protocols • protocols related to ownership and use of First Peoples oral texts				X		
Text features and structures • narrative structures, including those found in First Peoples texts • form, function, and genre of texts	X	X		X		
Strategies and processes • reading strategies • metacognitive strategies • writing processes • oral language strategies	X	X	X	X	X	X
Language features, structures, and conventions • elements of style • usage and conventions • literary elements and devices • citations and acknowledgements • literal and inferential meaning	X	X				

BRITISH COLUMBIA: ENGLISH FIRST PEOPLES: LITERARY STUDIES + SPOKEN LANGUAGE 11

Curricular Competencies [12] Using oral, written, visual, and digital texts, students are expected individually and collaboratively to be able to:	Lesson					
	1	2	3	4	5	6
Demonstrate understanding of how First Peoples languages and texts reflect their cultures, knowledge, histories, and worldviews		X	X	X		X
Access information for diverse purposes and from a variety of sources to inform development of oral texts		X	X	X		X
Apply appropriate strategies in a variety of contexts to guide inquiry, extend thinking, and comprehend oral and other texts	X	X	X	X	X	X
Recognize and appreciate how different forms, formats, structures, and features of texts reflect different purposes, audiences, and messages	X	X	X	X	X	X
Think critically, creatively, and reflectively to explore ideas within, between, and beyond texts	X	X	X	X	X	X
Recognize and identify personal, social, and cultural contexts, values, and perspectives in oral and other texts, including gender, sexual orientation, and socioeconomic factors		X	X	X	X	X
Demonstrate understanding of how language constructs and reflects personal, social, and cultural identities	X	X	X	X	X	X
Construct meaningful personal connections between self, text, and world	X	X	X	X	X	X
Recognize and understand the roles of story and oral traditions in expressing First Peoples perspectives, values, beliefs, and points of view		X	X	X		X
Understand and evaluate how literary elements, techniques, and devices enhance and shape meaning and impact	X	X	X	X		X
Recognize and understand the diversity within and across First Peoples societies as represented in texts		X	X	X	X	X
Assess the authenticity of First Peoples texts				X		
Understand the influence of land/place in First Peoples oral and other texts				X		X
Identify bias, contradictions, distortions, and omissions				X		

12 Based on *BC's Curriculum: English First Peoples Literary Studies + Spoken Language 11.* https://curriculum.gov.bc.ca/curriculum/english-language-arts/11/efp-literary-studies-and-spoken-language

Respectfully exchange ideas and viewpoints from diverse perspectives to build shared understandings and extend thinking		X	X	X		X
Demonstrate speaking and listening skills in a variety of formal and informal contexts for a range of purposes		X	X	X	X	X
Select and apply appropriate spoken language formats for intended purposes	X	X	X	X		X
Express and support an opinion with evidence	X	X	X	X		X
Respond to text in personal, creative, and critical ways	X	X	X	X	X	X
Use writing and design processes to plan, develop, and create engaging and meaningful texts for a variety of purposes and audiences	X	X	X	X		X
Use creative processes to plan, develop, and create engaging and meaningful oral texts for a variety of purposes and audiences		X	X	X		X
Assess and refine oral and other texts to improve clarity, effectiveness, and impact		X	X	X		X
Use a variety of techniques to engage listeners	X			X		X
Experiment with genres, forms, or styles of oral and other texts	X	X	X	X		X
Recognize intellectual property rights and community protocols and apply them as necessary				X		
Content Students are expected to know the following:						
A wide variety of BC, Canadian, and global First Peoples texts	X	X	X	X		
A wide variety of text forms and genres	X	X	X	X		
Common themes in First Peoples texts	X	X	X	X		
Reconciliation in Canada			X	X		X
First Peoples oral traditions • the legal status of First Peoples oral traditions in Canada • purposes of oral texts • the relationship between oral tradition and land/place				X		
Protocols • protocols related to the ownership and use of First Peoples oral texts • acknowledgement of territory • situating oneself in relation to others and place • processes related to protocols and expectations when engaging with First Nations communities and Aboriginal organizations		X	X	X		

Text features and structures • narrative structures, including those found in First Peoples texts • form, function, and genre of oral and other texts	X	X	X	X		
Strategies and processes • reading strategies • oral language strategies • metacognitive strategies • writing processes • oral storytelling techniques • presentation and performance strategies	X	X	X	X	X	X
Language features, structures, and conventions • features of oral language • elements of style • syntax and fluency • rhetorical devices • usage and conventions • literary elements and devices • literal and inferential meaning • persuasive techniques • citations and acknowledgements	X	X	X	X	X	X

BRITISH COLUMBIA: ENGLISH FIRST PEOPLES 12

Curricular Competencies [13] Using oral, written, visual, and digital texts, students are expected individually and collaboratively to be able to:	**Lesson**					
	1	**2**	**3**	**4**	**5**	**6**
Analyze how First Peoples languages and texts reflect their cultures, knowledge, histories, and worldviews		X	X	X		
Access information for diverse purposes and from a variety of sources and evaluate its relevance, accuracy, and reliability		X	X	X	X	X
Select and apply appropriate strategies in a variety of contexts to guide inquiry, extend thinking, and comprehend texts	X	X	X	X	X	X
Analyze how different forms, formats, structures, and features of texts reflect a variety of purposes, audiences, and messages	X	X	X	X	X	X
Think critically, creatively, and reflectively to explore ideas within, between, and beyond texts	X	X	X	X	X	X

13 Based on *BC's Curriculum: English First Peoples 12*. https://curriculum.gov.bc.ca/curriculum/english-language-arts/12/english-first-peoples

Recognize and identify personal, social, and cultural contexts, values, and perspectives in texts, including gender, sexual orientation, and socioeconomic factors		X	X	X	X	X
Appreciate and understand how language constructs and reflects personal, social, and cultural identities	X	X	X	X	X	X
Construct meaningful personal connections between self, text, and world	X	X	X	X	X	X
Demonstrate understanding of the role of story and oral traditions in expressing First Peoples perspectives, values, beliefs, and points of view		X	X	X		X
Understand and evaluate how literary elements, techniques, and devices enhance and shape meaning and impact	X	X	X	X		X
Analyze the diversity within and across First Peoples societies as represented in texts		X	X	X		X
Assess the authenticity of First Peoples texts				X		
Analyze the influence of land/place in First Peoples texts				X		X
Examine the significance of terms/words from First Peoples languages used in English texts				X		
Discern nuances in the meanings of words, considering social, political, historical, and literary contexts		X	X	X		
Identify bias, contradictions, distortions, and omissions				X		
Respectfully exchange ideas and viewpoints from diverse perspectives to build shared understandings and extend thinking		X	X	X		X
Demonstrate speaking and listening skills in a variety of formal and informal contexts for a range of purposes		X	X	X	X	X
Select and apply appropriate spoken language formats for intended purposes	X	X	X	X		X
Express and support an opinion with evidence	X	X	X	X		X
Respond to text in personal, creative, and critical ways	X	X	X	X	X	X
Use writing and design processes to plan, develop, and create engaging and meaningful texts for a variety of purposes and audiences	X	X	X	X		X
Assess and refine texts to improve clarity, effectiveness, and impact		X	X	X		X
Experiment with genres, forms, or styles of oral and other texts	X	X	X	X		X

Transform ideas and information to create original texts, using various genres, forms, structures, and styles	X	X	X	X		
Recognize intellectual property rights and community protocols and apply them as necessary				X		
Content Students are expected to know the following:						
A wide variety of BC, Canadian, and global First Peoples texts	X	X	X			
A wide variety of text forms and genres	X	X	X	X		
Common themes in First Peoples texts	X	X	X	X		
Reconciliation in Canada			X	X		X
First Peoples oral traditions • the legal status of First Peoples oral traditions in Canada • purposes of oral texts • the relationship between oral tradition and land/place				X		
Protocols • protocols related to the ownership and use of First Peoples oral texts • acknowledgement of territory • situating oneself in relation to others and place • processes related to protocols and expectations when engaging with First Nations communities and Aboriginal organizations		X	X	X		
Text features and structures • narrative structures, including those found in First Peoples texts • form, function, and genre of oral and other texts • elements of visual/graphic texts	X	X	X	X		
Strategies and processes • reading strategies • oral language strategies • metacognitive strategies • writing processes • presentation techniques	X	X	X	X	X	X
Language features, structures, and conventions • features of oral language • elements of style • language choice • syntax and sentence fluency • rhetorical devices • usage and conventions • literary elements and devices • literal and inferential meaning • persuasive techniques • citations and acknowledgements	X	X	X	X	X	X

MANITOBA: SENIOR 1 ENGLISH LANGUAGE ARTS

Curricular Outcomes [14]	Lesson					
	1	2	3	4	5	6
1.1.1 Express Ideas Question and reflect on personal responses, predictions, and interpretations; apply personal viewpoints to diverse situations or circumstances.	X	X	X	X		X
1.1.2 Consider Others' Ideas Acknowledge the value of others' ideas and opinions in exploring and extending personal interpretations and viewpoints.	X	X	X	X	X	X
1.1.3 Experiment with Language and Form Use memorable language effectively and experiment with different personas for dynamic self-expression.	X	X	X	X		X
1.2.1 Develop Understanding Reflect on new understanding in relation to prior knowledge and identify gaps in personal knowledge.	X	X	X	X	X	X
1.2.2 Explain Opinions Review and refine personal viewpoints through reflection, feedback, and self-assessment.		X	X	X		X
1.2.4 Extend Understanding Consider diverse opinions, explore ambiguities, and assess whether new information clarifies understanding.		X	X	X		X
2.1.1 Prior Knowledge Analyze and explain connections between previous experiences, prior knowledge, and a variety of texts [including books].		X	X	X		X
2.1.2 Comprehension Strategies Use comprehension strategies [including recognizing main ideas and significant supporting details, and paraphrasing ideas] appropriate to the type of text and purpose; enhance understanding by rereading and discussing relevant passages.		X	X	X		X
2.1.3 Textual Cues Use textual cues and prominent organizational patterns within texts to construct and confirm meaning and interpret texts.	X	X	X	X		X
2.2.2 Connect Self, Texts, and Culture Examine how personal experiences, community traditions, and Canadian perspectives are presented in oral, literary, and media texts.	X	X	X	X		X

14 Based on the 1996 edition of *Senior 1 English Language Arts: Manitoba Curriculum Framework of Outcomes and Senior 1 Standards.* https://www.edu.gov.mb.ca/k12/cur/ela/docs/s1_framework/index.html

2.3.5 Create Original Texts Create original texts to communicate and demonstrate understanding of forms and techniques.	X	X	X	X	X	
3.1.3 Participate in Group Inquiry Generate and access ideas in a group and use a variety of methods to focus and clarify inquiry or research topic.				X		X
3.3.1 Organize Information Organize information and ideas by developing and selecting appropriate categories and organizational structures.	X	X	X	X	X	X
3.3.2 Record Information Summarize and record information in a variety of forms in own words, paraphrasing and/or quoting relevant facts and opinions; reference sources.	X			X		X
4.2.2 Revise Content Analyze and revise drafts to ensure appropriate content, accuracy, clarity, and completeness.	X	X	X	X	X	X
4.2.3 Enhance Legibility Use appropriate text features to enhance legibility for particular audiences, purposes, and contexts.	X			X		X
4.3.1 Grammar and Usage Edit for parallel structure, use of transitional devices, and clarity.	X		X	X		X
4.3.2 Spelling Know and apply a repertoire of spelling conventions when editing and proofreading; use a variety of resources when editing and proofreading.	X		X	X		X
4.3.3 Capitalization and Punctuation Know and apply capitalization and punctuation conventions in dialogues, quotations, footnotes, endnotes, and references when editing and proofreading.	X		X	X		X
4.4.2 Effective Oral Communication Choose vocabulary, voice production factors, and nonverbal cues to communicate effectively to a variety of audiences; use a variety of media and display techniques to enhance the effectiveness of oral presentations.		X	X	X		X
5.1.1 Cooperate with Others Recognize the importance of effective communication in working with others.		X	X			X
5.1.2 Work in Groups Plan, organize, and participate in presentations of group findings.		X	X			X
5.2.1 Compare Responses Recognize that differing perspectives and unique reactions enrich understanding.	X	X	X	X		X

MANITOBA: SENIOR 2 ENGLISH LANGUAGE ARTS

Curriculum Outcomes [15]	Lesson					
	1	2	3	4	5	6
1.1.1 Express Ideas Consider the potential of emerging ideas through a variety of means to develop tentative positions.	X	X	X	X		X
1.1.3 Experiment with Language and Form Demonstrate a willingness to take risks in language use and experiment with language and forms of expression.	X	X	X	X		X
1.2.2 Explain Opinions Explain opinions, providing support or reasons; anticipate other viewpoints.		X		X		X
1.2.4 Extend Understanding Explore ways in which real and vicarious experiences and various perspectives affect understanding when generating and responding to texts.		X	X	X		X
2.1.1 Prior Knowledge Apply personal experiences and prior knowledge of language and texts to develop understanding and interpretations of a variety of texts [including books].	X	X	X	X	X	X
2.1.2 Comprehension Strategies Select, describe, and use comprehension strategies to monitor understanding and develop interpretations of a variety of texts.	X	X		X		X
2.1.3 Textual Cues Use textual cues and prominent organizational patterns to construct and confirm meaning and interpret texts.	X	X		X		X
2.2.2 Connect Self, Texts, and Culture Respond personally and critically to individuals, events, and ideas presented in a variety of Canadian and international texts.	X	X	X	X	X	X
3.1.3 Participate in Group Inquiry Collaborate to determine group knowledge base and to define research or inquiry purpose and parameters.						X
3.3.1 Organize Information Organize information using appropriate forms for specific purposes.	X	X	X	X	X	X

15 Based on the 1998 edition of *Senior 2 English Language Arts: Manitoba Curriculum Framework of Outcomes*. https://www.edu.gov.mb.ca/k12/cur/ela/docs/s2_framework/index.html

3.3.2 Record Information Select and record important information and ideas using an organizational structure appropriate for purpose and information source; document sources accurately.	X	X	X	X	X	X
4.2.2 Revise Content Analyze and revise drafts to ensure appropriate content, accuracy, clarity, and completeness.	X	X	X	X	X	X
4.2.3 Enhance Legibility Use appropriate text features to enhance legibility for particular audiences, purposes, and contexts.	X		X	X		X
4.3.1 Grammar and Usage Select appropriate words, grammatical structures, and register to achieve clarity and desired effect.	X		X	X		X
4.3.2 Spelling Know and apply Canadian spelling conventions for familiar and new vocabulary; monitor for correctness in editing and proofreading using appropriate resources.	X		X	X		X
4.3.3 Capitalization and Punctuation Know and apply capitalization and punctuation conventions to clarify intended meaning, using appropriate resources as required.	X		X	X		X
4.4.2 Effective Oral Communication Use appropriate voice production factors and non-verbal cues to clarify intent in personal and public communication.		X	X	X		X
5.1.1 Cooperate with Others Make and encourage contributions to assist in developing group ideas; take responsibility for developing and expressing viewpoints.		X	X			X
5.1.2 Work in Groups Demonstrate effective group interaction skills and strategies.		X	X			X
5.2.1 Compare Responses Consider various ideas, evidence, and viewpoints to expand understanding of texts, others, and self.	X	X	X	X		X

MANITOBA: SENIOR 3 ENGLISH LANGUAGE ARTS

Curriculum Outcomes [16]	Lesson					
	1	2	3	4	5	6
1.1.1 Express Ideas Connect ideas, observations, opinions, and emotions through a variety of means to develop a train of thought and test tentative positions.	X	X	X	X	X	X
1.1.3 Experiment with Language and Form Experiment with language and forms of expression to achieve particular effects.	X	X	X	X		X
1.2.2 Explain Opinions Explore various viewpoints and consider the consequences of particular positions when generating and responding to texts.		X		X		X
1.2.4 Extend Understanding Extend understanding by exploring and acknowledging multiple perspectives and ambiguities when generating and responding to texts.		X	X	X		X
2.1.1 Prior Knowledge Examine connections between personal experiences and prior knowledge of language and texts to develop understanding and interpretations of a variety of texts [including books].	X	X	X	X		X
2.1.2 Comprehension Strategies Use and adjust comprehension strategies to monitor understanding and develop interpretations of a variety of texts.	X	X		X		X
2.1.3 Textual Cues Use textual cues and prominent organizational patterns to construct and confirm meaning and interpret texts.	X	X		X		X
2.2.2 Connect Self, Texts, and Culture Respond personally and critically to ideas and values presented in a variety of Canadian and international texts.	X	X	X	X	X	X
2.3.5 Create Original Texts Create original texts to communicate ideas and enhance understanding of forms and techniques.	X	X	X	X		X
3.1.3 Participate in Group Inquiry Explore group knowledge and strengths to determine inquiry or research topic, purpose, and procedures.						X

16 Based on the 1999 edition of *Senior 3 English Language Arts: Manitoba Curriculum Framework of Outcomes*. https://www.edu.gov.mb.ca/k12/cur/ela/docs/s3_framework/index.html

3.3.1 Organize Information Organize and reorganize information and ideas in a variety of ways for different audiences and purposes.	X	X	X	X		X
3.3.2 Record Information Summarize and record information, ideas, and perspectives from a variety of sources; document sources accurately.	X	X	X	X		X
4.2.2 Revise Content Analyze and revise drafts to ensure appropriate content and to enhance unity, clarity, and coherence.	X	X	X	X		X
4.2.3 Enhance Legibility Use appropriate text features to enhance legibility for particular audiences, purposes, and contexts.	X		X	X		X
4.3.1 Grammar and Usage Select appropriate words, grammatical structures, and register for audience, purpose, and context.	X		X	X		X
4.3.2 Spelling Know and apply Canadian spelling conventions and monitor for correctness using appropriate resources; recognize adapted spellings for particular effects.	X		X	X		X
4.3.3 Capitalization and Punctuation Know and apply capitalization and punctuation conventions to clarify intended meaning, using appropriate resources as required.	X		X	X		X
4.4.2 Effective Oral Communication Use appropriate voice and visual production factors to communicate and emphasize intent in personal and public communication.	X	X	X	X		X
5.1.1 Cooperate with Others Use language to build and maintain collaborative relationships; take responsibility for respectfully questioning others' viewpoints and requesting further explanation.		X	X			X
5.1.2 Work in Groups Demonstrate effective group interaction skills and strategies.		X	X			X
5.2.1 Compare Responses Consider various ideas, evidence, and viewpoints to expand understanding of texts, others, and self.	X	X	X	X		X

MANITOBA: SENIOR 4 ENGLISH LANGUAGE ARTS

Curriculum Outcomes [17]	Lesson					
	1	2	3	4	5	6
1.1.1 Express Ideas Connect ideas, observations, opinions, and emotions through a variety of means to develop a train of thought and test tentative positions.	X	X	X	X		X
1.1.3 Experiment with Language and Form Experiment with language and forms of expression to achieve particular effects.	X	X	X	X		X
1.2.2 Explain Opinions Explore various viewpoints and consider the consequences of particular positions when generating and responding to texts.	X	X	X	X		X
1.2.4 Extend Understanding Extend understanding by exploring and acknowledging multiple perspectives and ambiguities when generating and responding to texts.	X	X	X	X		X
2.1.1 Prior Knowledge Examine connections between personal experiences and prior knowledge of language and texts to develop understanding and interpretations of a variety of texts [including books].	X	X	X	X	X	X
2.1.2 Comprehension Strategies Use and adjust comprehension strategies to monitor understanding and develop interpretations of a variety of texts.	X	X	X	X		X
2.1.3 Textual Cues Use textual cues and prominent organizational patterns to construct and confirm meaning and interpret texts.	X	X	X	X		X
2.2.2 Connect Self, Texts, and Culture Respond personally and critically to ideas and values presented in a variety of Canadian and international texts.	X	X	X	X	X	X
2.3.5 Create Original Texts Create original texts to communicate ideas and enhance understanding of forms and techniques.	X	X	X	X		X
3.1.3 Participate in Group Inquiry Explore group knowledge and strengths to determine inquiry or research topic, purpose, and procedures.						X

17 Based on the 2000 edition of *Senior 4 English Language Arts: Manitoba Curriculum Framework of Outcomes and Senior 4 Standards.* https://www.edu.gov.mb.ca/k12/cur/ela/docs/s4_framework/index.html

3.3.1 Organize Information Organize and reorganize information and ideas in a variety of ways for different audiences and purposes.	X	X	X	X		X
3.3.2 Record Information Summarize and record information, ideas, and perspectives from a variety of sources; document sources accurately.	X	X	X	X		X
4.2.2 Revise Content Analyze and revise drafts to ensure appropriate content and to enhance unity, clarity, and coherence.	X	X	X	X	X	X
4.2.3 Enhance Legibility Use appropriate text features to enhance legibility for particular audiences, purposes, and contexts.	X		X	X		X
4.3.1 Grammar and Usage Select appropriate words, grammatical structures, and register for audience, purpose, and context.	X		X	X		X
4.3.2 Spelling Know and apply Canadian spelling conventions and monitor for correctness using appropriate resources; recognize adapted spellings for particular effects.	X		X	X		X
4.3.3 Capitalization and Punctuation Know and apply capitalization and punctuation conventions to clarify intended meaning, using appropriate resources as required.	X		X	X		X
4.4.2 Effective Oral Communication Use appropriate voice and visual production factors to communicate and emphasize intent in personal and public communication.	X	X	X	X		X
5.1.1 Cooperate with Others Use language to build and maintain collaborative relationships; take responsibility for respectfully questioning others' viewpoints and requesting further explanation.		X	X	X		X
5.1.2 Work in Groups Demonstrate flexibility in assuming a variety of group roles and take responsibility for tasks that achieve group goals.		X	X			X
5.2.1 Compare Responses Identify various factors that shape understanding of texts, others, and self.		X	X			X

  ISBN: 978-1-77492-140-1

MANITOBA: GRADE 12 GLOBAL ISSUES: CITIZENSHIP AND SUSTAINABILITY

Curriculum Outcomes [18]	Lesson					
	1	2	3	4	5	6
Learning to Know *Acquire knowledge and understanding, and think critically about our complex and changing world.*						
Seek knowledge from diverse sources and perspectives.						X
Conduct focused in-depth inquiry.						X
Learning to Do *Learn to participate effectively in local, national, and global communities.*						
Engage in intercultural dialogue and cultivate a widening circle of empathy and concern.		X	X			X
Take Action						
Explore Indigenous perspectives to extend the boundaries of the familiar and to challenge assumptions and practices.		X	X			X
Area of Inquiry: Indigenous Peoples						
Inquire about the legacy of colonialism, colonization, and decolonization.						X
Inquire about the effects of enculturation, assimilation, and cultural loss for Indigenous Peoples.						X
Inquire about the impact of development and globalization on Indigenous Peoples, cultural homogenization, and the disappearance of Indigenous Peoples and cultures.						X
Inquire about the preservation of traditional Indigenous cultures and languages.						X
Inquire about the recognition of distinctive Indigenous worldviews and values.						X

18 Based on the 2017 edition of *Grade 12 Global Issues: Citizenship and Sustainability*. https://www.edu.gov.mb.ca/k12/cur/socstud/global_issue

  ISBN: 978-1-77492-140-1

MANITOBA: GRADE 12 CURRENT TOPICS IN FIRST NATIONS, MÉTIS, AND INUIT STUDIES

Curriculum Outcomes [19]	Lesson					
	1	2	3	4	5	6
1.1 Learn about the colonialist history of Canada and the impact of colonization on First Nations, Métis, and Inuit peoples in Canada.		X	X			X
1.2 Explore Indigenous identity from the viewpoint of First Nations, Métis, and Inuit peoples.		X	X	X	X	X
1.3 Examine contemporary mainstream Canadian society's perception of Indigenous people as "the other."		X	X			X
2.1 Investigate the historic, political, and economic practices of Indigenous peoples in Canada, before and after the arrival of Europeans.						X
2.3 Examine the historic and contemporary significance of the Indian Act, including the paradox that it is at once discriminatory and racist while it also preserves the sanctity of reserve lands.						X
3.3 Examine traditional Indigenous concepts and practices of justice, as well as the impact of colonization and the imposition of a western judicial model on First Nations, Métis, and Inuit peoples.						X
5.1 Work independently as individuals or with a partner or small group to create a project focusing on a theme relevant to contemporary Indigenous culture.						X

19 Based on the 2011 edition of *Grade 12 Current Topics in First Nations, Métis, and Inuit Studies: A Foundation for Implementation.* https://www.edu.gov.mb.ca/k12/abedu/foundation_gr12/full_doc.pdf

  ISBN: 978-1-77492-140-1

ONTARIO: GRADE 7 AND 8 LANGUAGE[20] AND GRADE 9 ENGLISH[21]

Strand A. Literacy Connections and Applications		Lesson					
Overall Expectations	**Specific Expectations**	**1**	**2**	**3**	**4**	**5**	**6**
A2. Digital Media Literacy demonstrate and apply the knowledge and skills needed to interact safely and responsibly in online environments, use digital and media tools to construct knowledge, and demonstrate learning as critical consumers and creators of media	**A2.4** evaluate the use of the various forms, conventions, and techniques of digital and media texts, consider the impact on the audience, and apply this understanding when analyzing and creating texts	X	X				
	A2.5 demonstrate an understanding of the interrelationships between the form, message, and context of texts, the intended and unintended audience, and the purpose for production	X	X				
A3. Applications, Connections, and Contributions apply language and literacy skills in cross-curricular and integrated learning, and demonstrate an understanding of, and make connections to, diverse voices, experiences, perspectives, histories, and contributions, including those of First Nations, Métis, and Inuit individuals, communities, groups, and nations	**A3.1** analyze and explain how the knowledge and skills developed in this grade support learning in various subject areas and in everyday life, and describe how they enhance understanding and communication	X	X				
	A3.2 demonstrate an understanding of the historical contexts, contributions, lived experiences, and perspectives of a diversity of individuals and communities, including those in Canada, by exploring and analyzing the concepts of identity, self, and sense of belonging in a variety of culturally responsive and relevant texts		X	X	X	X	X
	A3.3 analyze themes explored in First Nations, Métis, and Inuit cultures to demonstrate an understanding of the varied identities, perspectives, relationships, legacies, truths, and ways of knowing, being, and doing		X	X	X	X	X

20 Based on *The Ontario Curriculum, Grades 1–8: Language, 2023*. https://www.dcp.edu.gov.on.ca/en/curriculum/elementary-language

21 Based on *The Ontario Curriculum, Grade 9: English, 2023*. https://www.dcp.edu.gov.on.ca/en/curriculum/secondary-english/courses/enl1w/home

Strand B. Foundations of Language							
B1. Oral and Non-Verbal Communication apply listening, speaking, and non-verbal communication skills and strategies to understand and communicate meaning in formal and informal contexts and for various purposes and audiences	**B1.1** analyze various effective listening skills, including understanding when to ask relevant questions and how to respond to the contributions of others in group discussions, and use these skills in formal and informal contexts and for various purposes			X	X		
	B1.2 select and use a variety of listening strategies before, during, and after listening to comprehend information communicated orally and non-verbally, seek clarification, and develop a relevant response appropriate to the context			X	X		
	B1.3 identify the purpose and audience for speaking in formal and informal contexts, and choose appropriate speaking strategies to communicate clearly and coherently			X	X		
	B1.4 identify and use oral and non-verbal communication strategies, including expression, gestures, and body language, and analyze the ways in which these strategies support understanding or communication, including how their use may vary across cultures			X	X		
	B1.5 use precise and descriptive word choice, including varied adjectives and adverbs to elaborate, a variety of sentence types, cohesive and coherent sentences, and the active or passive voice as appropriate during formal and informal communication, to support audience comprehension			X	X		

  ISBN: 978-1-77492-140-1

Strand C. Comprehension: Understanding and Responding to Texts							
C1. Knowledge about Texts apply foundational knowledge and skills to understand a variety of texts, including digital and media texts, by creators with diverse identities, perspectives, and experience, and demonstrate an understanding of the patterns, features, and elements of style associated with various text forms and genres	**C1.1** read and comprehend various complex texts, using knowledge of words, grammar, cohesive ties, sentence structures, and background knowledge	X	X	X	X		X
	C1.2 analyze a variety of text forms and genres, including cultural text forms, and explain how their characteristics help communicate meaning	X	X	X	X		X
	C1.3 analyze text patterns, such as cause and effect in an expository text, and text features, such as a bibliography and accessible fonts, associated with various text forms, including cultural texts, and explain how they help readers, listeners, and viewers understand the meaning	X	X	X	X		X
	C1.4 analyze and compare how images, graphics, and visual design create, communicate, and contribute to meaning in a variety of texts	X	X	X	X		X
	C1.5 identify various elements of style in texts, including voice, word choice, word patterns, and sentence structure, and analyze how each element helps create meaning and is appropriate for the text form and genre	X	X	X	X		X
	C1.6 identify the narrator's point of view, including first, second, or third person, in a variety of texts, providing evidence, and explain how using an alternative point of view would change each story						
	C1.7 read, listen to, and view various forms of texts by diverse First Nations, Métis, and Inuit creators to make meaning through Indigenous Storywork about First Nations, Métis, and Inuit histories, cultures, relationships, communities, groups, nations, and lived experiences	X	X	X	X	X	X

C2. Comprehension Strategies apply comprehension strategies before, during, and after reading, listening to, and viewing a variety of texts, including digital and media texts, by creators with diverse identities, perspectives, and experience, in order to understand and clarify the meaning of texts	**C2.1** identify and explain prior knowledge from various sources, including personal experiences and learning in other subject areas, that they can use to make connections and understand new texts	X	X	X	X	X	X
	C2.2 identify a variety of purposes for engaging with texts, select texts from diverse creators that are suitable for the purposes, and explain why the selections are appropriate	X					
	C2.4 select suitable strategies, such as visualizing, reading ahead, asking questions, and consulting references and other texts or sources of information, to monitor and confirm their understanding of various texts and solve comprehension problems	X	X	X	X		X
	C2.5 explain how the ideas expressed in texts connect to their knowledges and lived experiences, the ideas in other texts, and the world around them	X	X	X	X	X	X
C3. Critical Thinking in Literacy apply critical thinking skills to deepen understanding of texts, and analyze how various perspectives and topics are communicated and addressed in a variety of texts, including digital, media, and cultural texts	**C3.3** analyze complex texts, including literary and informational texts, by evaluating, synthesizing, and sequencing relevant information and formulating conclusions	X	X	X			
	C3.4 analyze cultural elements that are represented in various texts, including values, rituals and ceremonies, architecture, art, and dance, by investigating the meanings of these elements, making connections to their lived experience and culture, and sharing their interpretations with others	X	X	X	X	X	X
	C3.6 explain how various topics, such as diversity, inclusion, and accessibility, are addressed in texts, analyze the insights or messages conveyed, and identify different positions presented	X	X	X	X		X
	C3.7 assess the influence of historical periods, cultural experiences, and/or socio-political conditions and events on texts created by First Nations, Métis, and Inuit individuals, communities, groups, or nations, and how they relate to current lived experiences						X
	C3.8 compare the critical thinking skills they used when analyzing and evaluating various texts, identify the skills that best supported their understanding, and explain why they were effective	X	X	X	X		X

Strand D. Composition: Expressing Ideas and Creating Texts							
D1. Developing Ideas and Organizing Content plan, develop ideas, gather information, and organize content for creating texts of various forms, including digital and media texts, on a variety of topics	**D1.1** identify the topic, purpose, and audience for various texts they plan to create, and analyze why the chosen text form, genre, and medium suit the purpose and audience, and how they will help communicate the intended meaning	X	X				
	D1.2 generate and develop ideas and details about various topics, such as topics related to diversity, equity, and inclusion and to other subject areas, using a variety of strategies, and drawing on various resources, including their own lived experiences	X	X	X	X		X
	D1.3 gather and synthesize information and content relevant to a topic, using a variety of textual sources and appropriate strategies; evaluate the quality, bias, and accuracy of information; verify the reliability of sources; and record the creator and source of all content created by others						X
	D1.4 classify and sequence ideas and collected information, using appropriate strategies and tools, and identify and organize relevant content, taking into account the chosen text form, genre, and medium	X	X	X			
	D1.5 explain and compare how the strategies and tools used helped them develop ideas and organize content for texts of the chosen forms, genres, and media, and how they helped them improve as a text creator	X	X	X			

D2. Creating Texts apply knowledge and understanding of various text forms and genres to create, revise, edit, and proofread their own texts, using a variety of media, tools, and strategies, and reflect critically on created texts	**D2.1** draft complex texts of various forms and genres, including narrative, expository, and informational texts, using a variety of media, tools, and strategies	X	X	X	X		
	D2.3 establish a personal voice in their texts, using language and elements of style to express their thoughts, feelings, and opinions about a topic, and using a tone appropriate to the form and genre		X				
	D2.4 identify the point of view, perspectives, and bias conveyed in their texts, and explain how their messages might be interpreted by audiences with different perspectives	X	X	X			
	D2.5 make revisions to the content, elements of style, patterns, and features of draft texts, and add, delete and re-sequence sentences to improve clarity, focus, and coherence, using various strategies and seeking and selectively using feedback	X	X	X	X		
	D2.6 edit draft texts to improve accuracy and style, checking for errors in spelling, punctuation, grammar, and format; edit digital texts using word-processing software, including spell- and grammar-checkers	X	X	X	X		
D3. Publishing, Presenting, and Reflecting select suitable and effective media, techniques, and tools to publish and present final texts, and critically analyze how well the texts address various topics	**D3.1** produce final texts, selecting a variety of suitable techniques and tools, including digital design and production tools, to achieve the intended effect		X	X	X		
	D3.2 publish and present texts they have created, using various media and tools, and analyze how their choices helped them communicate their intended message				X		
	D3.3 compare how various strategies and tools helped them communicate their intended message when publishing and presenting texts, analyze how their texts address various topics, and suggest steps for future improvement as a text creator				X		

  ISBN: 978-1-77492-140-1

ONTARIO: GRADE 10 ENGLISH LANGUAGE ARTS (ACADEMIC)

Curriculum Outcomes [22]	Lesson					
	1	2	3	4	5	6
Listen to Understand By the end of this course, students will:						
1.2 select and use appropriate active listening strategies when participating in a variety of classroom interactions	X	X	X	X	X	X
Speaking to Communicate By the end of this course, students will:						
2.1 communicate orally for a variety of purposes, using language appropriate for the intended audience		X	X	X		X
2.2 demonstrate an understanding of a variety of interpersonal speaking strategies and adapt them to suit the purpose, situation, and audience, exhibiting sensitivity to cultural differences		X	X	X		X
2.3 communicate in a clear, coherent manner, using a structure and style appropriate to the purpose, subject matter, and intended audience		X	X	X		X

ONTARIO: GRADE 11 ENGLISH LANGUAGE ARTS (UNIVERSITY PREP)

Curriculum Outcomes [23]	Lesson					
	1	2	3	4	5	6
Developing and Organizing Content By the end of this course, students will:						
1.2 generate and focus ideas for potential writing tasks, using several different strategies and print, electronic, and other resources, as appropriate	X	X	X	X		X
1.3 locate and select information to support ideas for writing, using several different strategies and print, electronic, and other resources, as appropriate				X		X
1.4 identify, sort, and order main ideas and supporting details for writing tasks, using several different strategies and organizational patterns suited to the content and purpose for writing			X	X		X

22 Based on the 2007 edition of *The Ontario Curriculum, Grades 9 and 10: English.* http://www.edu.gov.on.ca/eng/curriculum/secondary/english910currb.pdf

23 Based on the 2007 edition of *The Ontario Curriculum, Grades 11 and 12: English.* http://www.edu.gov.on.ca/eng/curriculum/secondary/english1112currb.pdf

Speaking to Communicate By the end of this course, students will:						
2.1 communicate orally for several different purposes, using language suitable for the intended audience		X	X	X		X
2.2 demonstrate an understanding of a variety of interpersonal speaking strategies and adapt them to suit the purpose, situation, and audience, exhibiting sensitivity to cultural differences		X	X	X		X
2.3 communicate in a clear, coherent manner, using a structure and style effective for the purpose, subject matter, and intended audience		X	X	X		X

ONTARIO: GRADE 11 ENGLISH LANGUAGE ARTS (READING AND LITERATURE STUDIES)

Curriculum Outcomes [24]	Lesson					
	1	2	3	4	5	6
Reading for Meaning By the end of this course, students will:						
1.5 extend understanding of texts, including increasingly complex or difficult texts, by making appropriate and increasingly rich connections between the ideas in them and personal knowledge, experience, and insights; other texts; and the world around them		X	X	X		X
1.8 identify and analyze the perspectives and/or biases evident in texts, including increasingly complex or difficult texts, commenting with growing understanding on any questions they may raise about beliefs, values, identity, and power		X	X	X		
Understanding Form and Style By the end of this course, students will:						
2.1 identify a variety of characteristics of literary, informational, and graphic text forms and explain how they help communicate meaning	X	X	X			
Reading with Fluency By the end of this course, students will:						
3.5 proofread and correct their writing, using guidelines developed with the teacher and peers	X	X	X	X		

24 Based on the 2007 edition of *The Ontario Curriculum, Grades 11 and 12*: English. http://www.edu.gov.on.ca/eng/curriculum/secondary/english1112currb.pdf

ONTARIO: GRADE 12 ENGLISH LANGUAGE ARTS (UNIVERSITY PREP)

Curriculum Outcomes [25]	Lesson					
	1	2	3	4	5	6
Oral Communication By the end of this course, students will:						
1.1 identify the purpose of a wide range of listening tasks and set goals for specific tasks	X	X	X	X	X	X
Speaking to Communicate By the end of this course, students will:						
2.1 communicate orally for a wide range of purposes, using language effective for the intended audience	X	X	X	X		X
2.2 demonstrate an understanding of a variety of interpersonal speaking strategies and adapt them to suit the purpose, situation, and audience, exhibiting sensitivity to cultural differences	X	X	X	X	X	X
2.3 communicate in a clear, coherent manner, using a structure and style effective for the purpose, subject matter, and intended audience	X	X	X	X		X

ONTARIO: GRADE 12 ENGLISH LANGUAGE ARTS (READING AND LITERATURE STUDIES)

Curriculum Outcomes [26]	Lesson					
	1	2	3	4	5	6
Reading for Meaning By the end of this course, students will:						
1.5 extend understanding of texts, including complex and challenging texts, by making rich and increasingly insightful connections between the ideas in them and personal knowledge, experience, and insights; other texts; and the world around them	X	X	X			X
1.8 identify and analyze the perspectives and/or biases evident in texts, including complex and challenging texts, commenting with understanding and increasing insight on any questions they may raise about beliefs, values, identity, and power		X	X	X		X

25 Based on the 2007 edition of *The Ontario Curriculum, Grades 11 and 12: English.* http://www.edu.gov.on.ca/eng/curriculum/secondary/english1112currb.pdf

26 Based on the 2007 edition of *The Ontario Curriculum, Grades 11 and 12: English.* http://www.edu.gov.on.ca/eng/curriculum/secondary/english1112currb.pdf

	1	2	3	4	5	6
Understanding Form and Style By the end of this course, students will:						
2.1 identify a variety of characteristics of literary, informational, and graphic text forms and demonstrate insight into the way they help communicate meaning	X	X	X			
Reading with Fluency By the end of this course, students will:						
3.5 proofread and correct their writing, using guidelines developed with the teacher and peers	X	X	X	X	X	X

ONTARIO: GRADE 10 FIRST NATIONS, MÉTIS, AND INUIT IN CANADA[27]

Strand F. 1969 to the Present: Resilience, Determination, and Reconciliation		Lesson					
Overall Expectations	**Specific Expectations**	**1**	**2**	**3**	**4**	**5**	**6**
F1. Social, Economic, and Political Context describe some key social, economic, and political issues, trends, and developments that have affected Indigenous peoples in Canada from 1969 to the present, and analyse their impact	**F1.1** explain how some social trends, movements, and developments have affected Indigenous individuals and communities in Canada during this period, including in interactions with non-Indigenous Canadians						X
	F1.2 describe some key economic trends and developments that have affected Indigenous individuals and communities in Canada during this period, and analyse the impact on their lives						X
	F1.3 describe some key political trends and developments that have affected Indigenous individuals and communities in Canada during this period, and analyse the impact on their lives						X

27 Based on *The Ontario Curriculum, Grades 9 to 12: First Nations, Métis, and Inuit Studies (2019).* https://www.dcp.edu.gov.on.ca/en/curriculum/secondary-first-nations-metis-and-inuit-studies

F2. Communities, Conflict, and Cooperation analyse various legal and demographic developments involving Indigenous peoples in Canada, as well as responses to them, from 1969 to the present	**F2.1** identify some major trends and developments that have affected Indigenous individuals living off reserve in both rural and urban communities during this period, and assess their impact						X
	F2.2 analyse some key court cases related to Aboriginal title and/or treaty rights during this period, and assess their impact on Indigenous communities						X
	F2.3 describe some key treaties and land agreements between Canadian governments and First Nations and Inuit during this period						X
	F2.4 analyse historical and contemporary statistics and other sources to identify key demographic trends among First Nations, Métis, and Inuit populations during this period						X
	F2.5 describe some major instances of conflict involving Indigenous peoples in Canada during this period, and analyse some of their causes and consequences						X
F3. Identities, Cultures, and Self-Determination analyse how various individuals, groups, and issues have contributed to the development of Indigenous identities, cultures, and rights in Canada since 1969	**F3.1** describe some trends, issues, and/or developments that have affected Indigenous peoples globally during this period, and explain their impact on Indigenous peoples and non-Indigenous groups in Canada						X
	F3.2 analyse the contributions of some individuals and groups to efforts to raise awareness about sovereignty/self-governance and to gain recognition of Aboriginal title and/or treaty rights during this period						X
	F3.3 analyse actions taken by Indigenous individuals, communities, and/or organizations during this period in response to some developments that have had or could have a negative effect on the environment						X
	F3.4 describe some significant issues, trends, and developments in the arts and popular culture in Canada that are relevant to Indigenous peoples during this period, including the cultural contributions of some Indigenous individuals, and explain how these developments/contributions reflect and enhance First Nations, Métis, and Inuit identities						X

ONTARIO: GRADE 11 ENGLISH: UNDERSTANDING CONTEMPORARY FIRST NATIONS, MÉTIS, AND INUIT VOICES[28]

Strand A. First Nations, Métis, and Inuit Perspectives and Text Forms in Canada		**Lesson**					
Overall Expectations	**Specific Expectations**	**1**	**2**	**3**	**4**	**5**	**6**
A1. Exploring explore themes related to First Nations, Métis, and Inuit identities, relationships, and self-determination, sovereignty, or self-governance, as reflected in text forms created in Canada, formulating questions and comparing perspectives to stimulate a well-reasoned exchange of ideas about these topics	**A1.2** formulate increasingly effective questions to guide their explorations of themes, ideas, and issues related to First Nations, Métis, and Inuit identities, relationships, and self-determination, sovereignty, or self-governance, as reflected in various Indigenous text forms, and, as appropriate, in relevant non-Indigenous texts						X
	A1.3 identify and explain diverse themes, ideas, and issues related to First Nations, Métis, and Inuit identities, as reflected in various Indigenous text forms, and, as appropriate, in relevant non-Indigenous texts						X
	A1.4 identify and explain diverse themes, ideas, and issues associated with relationships in First Nations, Métis, and Inuit cultures, as reflected in various Indigenous text forms, and, as appropriate, in relevant non-Indigenous texts						X
	A1.5 identify and explain diverse themes, ideas, and issues related to First Nations, Métis, and Inuit self-determination, sovereignty, or self-governance, as reflected in various Indigenous text forms, and, as appropriate, in relevant non-Indigenous texts						X
	A1.6 compare multiple perspectives on themes, ideas, and issues related to First Nations, Métis, and Inuit identities, relationships, and self-determination, sovereignty, or self-governance, as reflected in various texts from both Indigenous and non-Indigenous sources						X

28 Based on *The Ontario Curriculum, Grades 9 to 12: First Nations, Métis, and Inuit Studies (2019).* https://www.dcp.edu.gov.on.ca/en/curriculum/secondary-first-nations-metis-and-inuit-studies

  ISBN: 978-1-77492-140-1

A3. Reconstructing demonstrate an understanding of the role of contemporary and historical text forms created in Canada in representing the diversity of First Nations, Métis, and Inuit lives, cultures, and world views, and assess the impact on Canadian society of efforts to challenge colonialist views and incomplete or inaccurate representations	**A3.1** demonstrate an understanding of the challenges First Nations, Métis, and Inuit individuals and communities face and have faced in controlling their own narratives and resisting colonialist views, as revealed in text forms studied in this course						X
	A3.2 identify appropriate ways to refer to Indigenous peoples in diverse contexts and locate examples of inappropriate terminology in contemporary and historical text forms from both Indigenous and non-Indigenous sources						X
	A3.4 evaluate a variety of contemporary text forms to determine how accurately they represent the lives and activities of First Nations, Métis, and Inuit individuals and communities, past and present						X
Strand C. Reading and Literature Studies							
C1. Reading for Meaning read and demonstrate an understanding of a variety of literary, informational, and graphic texts from First Nations, Métis, and Inuit cultures, and, as appropriate, relevant texts from non-Indigenous sources, using a range of strategies to construct meaning	**C1.1** read a variety of student- and teacher-selected contemporary texts from diverse First Nations, Métis, and Inuit cultures, and, as appropriate, relevant texts from non-Indigenous sources and historical texts, identifying specific purposes for reading	X	X	X	X		X
	C1.2 select and use the most appropriate reading comprehension strategies before, during, and after reading to understand texts from First Nations, Métis, and Inuit cultures, and, as appropriate, relevant texts from non-Indigenous sources, including increasingly complex or difficult texts	X	X	X	X		X
	C1.3 identify the most important ideas and supporting details in texts from First Nations, Métis, and Inuit cultures, and, as appropriate, in relevant texts from non-Indigenous sources, including increasingly complex or difficult texts	X	X	X	X		X
	C1.4 make and explain inferences of increasing subtlety about texts from First Nations, Métis, and Inuit cultures, and, as appropriate, relevant texts from non-Indigenous sources, including increasingly complex or difficult texts, supporting their explanations with well-chosen stated and implied ideas from the texts	X	X	X	X		X

  ISBN: 978-1-77492-140-1

C1. Reading for Meaning (continued)	**C1.5** extend their understanding of texts from First Nations, Métis, and Inuit cultures, and, as appropriate, relevant texts from non-Indigenous sources, including increasingly complex or difficult texts, by making rich connections between the ideas in them and in other texts and to their own knowledge, experience, and insights	X	X	X	X		X
	C1.6 analyse texts, including increasingly complex or difficult texts, in terms of the information, themes, ideas, and issues they explore in relation to First Nations, Métis, and Inuit cultures, explaining with increasing insight how various aspects of the texts contribute to the presentation or development of these elements	X	X	X	X		X
	C1.7 evaluate the effectiveness of texts from First Nations, Métis, and Inuit cultures, and, as appropriate, relevant texts from non-Indigenous sources, including increasingly complex or difficult texts, using evidence from the text to support their opinions	X	X	X	X		X
C2. Understanding Form and Style identify a variety of text forms, text features, and stylistic elements in texts from First Nations, Métis, and Inuit cultures, and, as appropriate, relevant texts from non-Indigenous sources, and demonstrate an understanding of how they help communicate meaning	**C2.1** identify a variety of characteristics of literary, informational, and graphic text forms, and explain, with increasing insight, how they help communicate meaning or reflect a world view	X	X	X	X		X
	C2.2 identify a variety of features of texts from First Nations, Métis, and Inuit cultures, and, as appropriate, relevant texts from non-Indigenous sources, and explain, with increasing insight, how they help communicate meaning or reflect a world view	X	X	X	X		X
	C2.3 identify a variety of elements of style in texts from First Nations, Métis, and Inuit cultures, and, as appropriate, in relevant texts from non-Indigenous sources, and explain, with increasing insight, how they help communicate meaning or reflect a world view and enhance the effectiveness of the text	X	X	X	X		X
C3. Reading with Fluency use knowledge of words and cueing systems to read fluently	**C3.1** demonstrate an automatic understanding of most words in a variety of reading contexts related to First Nations, Métis, and Inuit cultures	X	X	X	X		X
	C3.2 use decoding strategies effectively to read and understand unfamiliar words, including words of increasing difficulty, in texts from First Nations, Métis, and Inuit cultures, and, as appropriate, in relevant texts from non-Indigenous sources	X	X	X	X		X
	C3.3 use a variety of strategies, with increasing regularity, to explore and expand vocabulary	X	X	X	X		X

Strand D. Writing								
D1. Developing and Organizing Content generate, gather, and organize ideas and information to write for an intended purpose and audience on subject matter related to First Nations, Métis, and Inuit cultures	**D1.1** identify the topic, purpose, and audience for a variety of writing tasks on subject matter related to First Nations, Métis, and Inuit cultures	X	X	X	X		X
	D1.2 generate, expand, explore, and focus ideas for potential writing tasks, using a variety of strategies and print, electronic, and other resources, as appropriate and with increasing effectiveness	X	X	X	X		X
	D1.3 locate and select information to effectively support ideas for writing, using a variety of strategies and print, electronic, and other resources, as appropriate	X	X	X	X		X
	D1.5 determine whether the ideas and information gathered are accurate and complete, interesting, and effectively meet the requirements of the writing task	X	X	X	X		X
D2. Using Knowledge of Form and Style draft and revise their writing, using a variety of literary, informational, and graphic forms and stylistic elements appropriate for the purpose and audience	**D2.1** write for different purposes and audiences using a variety of literary, informational, and graphic text forms	X	X	X	X		X
	D2.2 establish a distinctive voice in their writing, modifying language and tone skillfully and effectively to suit the form, audience, and purpose for writing	X	X	X			
	D2.3 use appropriate descriptive and evocative words, phrases, and expressions imaginatively to make their writing clear, vivid, and interesting for their intended audience	X	X	X	X		X
	D2.4 write complete sentences that communicate their meaning clearly and effectively, skillfully varying sentence type, structure, and length to suit different purposes and making smooth and logical transitions between ideas	X	X	X	X		X
	D2.5 explain, with increasing insight, how their own beliefs, values, and experiences are revealed in their writing, and how these may either reflect or conflict with a First Nations, Métis, or Inuit world view	X	X	X	X	X	
	D2.6 revise drafts to improve the content, organization, clarity, and style of their written work, using a variety of teacher-modelled strategies with increasing effectiveness	X	X	X	X	X	X

D2. Using Knowledge of Form and Style (continued)	**D2.7** produce revised drafts of a variety of texts, including increasingly complex texts, written to meet criteria identified by the teacher, based on the curriculum expectations and respecting First Nations, Métis, and Inuit communication styles	X	X	X	X	X	X
D3. Applying Knowledge of Conventions use editing, proofreading, and publishing skills and strategies, and knowledge of language conventions, to correct errors, refine expression, and present their work effectively	**D3.1** consistently use knowledge of spelling rules and patterns, a variety of resources, and appropriate strategies to identify and correct their own and others' spelling errors	X	X	X	X	X	X
	D3.2 build vocabulary for writing by confirming word meaning(s) and reviewing and refining word choice, using a variety of resources and strategies, as appropriate for the purpose and with increasing effectiveness	X	X	X	X	X	X
	D3.3 use punctuation correctly and effectively to communicate their intended meaning	X	X	X	X	X	X
	D3.4 use grammar conventions correctly and appropriately to communicate their intended meaning clearly and effectively	X	X	X	X	X	X
	D3.5 regularly proofread and correct their writing	X	X	X	X	X	X
	D3.6 use a variety of presentation features, including print and script, fonts, graphics, and layout, to improve the clarity and coherence of their written work and to heighten its appeal and effectiveness for their audience	X	X	X			X
	D3.7 produce pieces of published work to meet criteria identified by the teacher, based on the curriculum expectations and respecting First Nations, Métis, and Inuit communication styles	X	X	X	X	X	X

Overall Expectations	Specific Expectations	1	2	3	4	5	6
D4. Reflecting on Skills and Strategies reflect on and identify their strengths as writers, areas for improvement, and the strategies they found most helpful at different stages of writing texts on subject matter related to First Nations, Métis, and Inuit cultures	**D4.1** explain which of a variety of strategies they found most helpful before, during, and after writing texts on subject matter related to First Nations, Métis, and Inuit cultures, then evaluate their areas of greater and lesser strength as writers and identify the steps they can take to improve their skills	X	X	X			
	D4.2 identify a variety of skills they have in listening, speaking, reading, viewing, and representing, and explain, with increasing insight, how these skills help them write texts on subject matter related to First Nations, Métis, and Inuit cultures more effectively	X	X	X	X		X
	D4.3 select examples of a variety of types of writing that express themes, ideas, and perspectives explored in this course and that they think most clearly reflect their growth and competence as writers, and explain the reasons for their choice	X	X	X	X	X	X

ONTARIO: GRADE 12 CONTEMPORARY INDIGENOUS ISSUES AND PERSPECTIVES IN A GLOBAL CONTEXT[29]

Strand A. Political Inquiry and Skill Development		**Lesson**					
Overall Expectations	**Specific Expectations**	**1**	**2**	**3**	**4**	**5**	**6**
A1. Political Inquiry use the political inquiry process and the concepts of political thinking when investigating contemporary issues, events, and developments relating to contemporary Indigenous peoples around the world	**A1.1** formulate different types of questions to guide investigations into contemporary issues, events, and/or developments relating to Indigenous peoples around the world						X
	A1.2 select and organize relevant evidence, data, and information on contemporary issues, events, and/or developments relating to Indigenous peoples around the world from a variety of primary and secondary sources, including Indigenous knowledge sources						X
	A1.3 assess the accuracy and credibility of sources relevant to their investigations						X

29 Based on *The Ontario Curriculum, Grades 9 to 12: First Nations, Métis, and Inuit Studies (2019).* https://www.dcp.edu.gov.on.ca/en/curriculum/secondary-first-nations-metis-and-inuit-studies

	A1.4 interpret and analyse evidence, data, and information relevant to their investigations, using various tools, strategies, and approaches appropriate for political inquiry						X
	A1.5 use the concepts of political thinking (i.e., political significance, objectives and results, stability and change, political perspective) when analysing, evaluating evidence about, and formulating conclusions and/or judgements regarding contemporary issues, events, and/or developments relating to Indigenous peoples around the world						X
A1. Political Inquiry (continued)	**A1.6** evaluate and synthesize their findings to formulate conclusions and make informed judgements or predictions about the issues, events, and/or developments they are investigating						X
	A1.7 communicate their ideas, arguments, and conclusions, using various formats and styles, as appropriate for the audience and purpose						X
	A1.8 use accepted forms of documentation to acknowledge all sources of information						X
	A1.9 assess and use terminology appropriate to the audience and purpose when communicating the results of their investigations						X
A2. Developing Transferable Skills apply, in a variety of contexts, skills developed through investigations related to contemporary Indigenous realities and perspectives in a global context, and identify careers in which the knowledge and skills acquired in this course might be an asset	**A2.1** describe several ways in which investigations related to contemporary Indigenous realities around the world can help them develop essential skills						X
	A2.2 demonstrate in everyday contexts attributes, skills, and work habits developed through investigations into contemporary Indigenous realities and perspectives in a global context						X
	A2.3 apply the concepts of political thinking when analysing current events relating to Indigenous peoples globally						X
	A2.4 identify various careers in the private and public sectors in which a background in global Indigenous perspectives and realities might be an asset						X

Overall Expectation	Specific Expectation						
B. Indigenous Peoples and Perspectives							
B1. Diversity and Identity demonstrate an understanding of the global diversity of Indigenous peoples and cultures, and of how Indigenous identity and diversity may be defined, affirmed, or denied, distinguishing between the sociocultural practices and world views of a variety of Indigenous peoples	**B1.1** analyse ways in which Indigenous identity and diversity may be defined, affirmed, or denied, drawing on evidence from a variety of cultures to support their conclusions	X	X	X	X	X	X
B2. Connections to the Land demonstrate an understanding of the significance of the land to Indigenous peoples around the world, analysing the consequences of displacement from traditional territories and the benefits of Indigenous perspectives on resource management	**B2.1** analyse the impact on Indigenous peoples of physical changes to and/or displacement from traditional lands, assessing the causes of change and the results of some contemporary efforts to address the consequences						X
	B2.2 explain the significance of Indigenous perspectives and practices for land stewardship and resource management in a global context identifying and describing some contemporary efforts to acknowledge these perspectives and follow these practices						X
B3. Indigenous Knowledge and Oral Traditions demonstrate an understanding of the role of Indigenous knowledge, storytelling, and storywork in fulfilling communal responsibilities, sustaining world views, and protecting cultural heritage	**B3.1** analyse the role of storytelling and storywork in the transmission of Indigenous knowledge, values, and identity, drawing on evidence from a variety of cultures to support their conclusions	X	X	X	X		
	B3.2 analyse the role of Indigenous knowledge in the protection and exercise of Indigenous community rights and responsibilities that are being challenged by global socio-economic trends						X
C. Global Trends and Cultural Survival							
C1. Economic, Social, and Technological Trends demonstrate an understanding of key global economic, social, and technological trends, issues, and developments related to the cultural survival of Indigenous peoples	**C1.1** analyse a variety of current economic trends, issues, and/or developments affecting the rights of Indigenous peoples around the world, including rights related to traditional lands and territories, water, and natural resources, to determine their connection to cultural survival						X
	C1.2 make and explain some connections between language use and cultural survival, drawing on evidence from Indigenous communities in several different countries						X

C1. Economic, Social, and Technological Trends (continued)	**C1.3** evaluate a variety of ways in which contemporary communications and information technologies, including social media, support or challenge the cultural survival of Indigenous communities						X
C2. Human Rights, Social Justice, and Cultural Survival demonstrate an understanding of various legal and social factors affecting the human rights of Indigenous peoples, including the role and rights of Indigenous women and children and the relationship between living conditions and human rights	**C2.1** describe key human rights challenges faced by Indigenous peoples around the world						X
	C2.2 analyse key global developments related to social justice for Indigenous peoples to determine their connection to human rights and cultural survival						X
	C2.3 analyse the role of Indigenous women and children in cultural survival, identifying various factors that necessitate the legal protection of their human rights						X
C3. Political Trends and Power Relations demonstrate an understanding of the connections between political power and cultural survival, analysing the balance of power in a variety of interactions between Indigenous and non-Indigenous groups	**C3.1** analyse a variety of current political trends, issues, and/or developments, including ways to address the continued impact of colonialism, in terms of their influence on the political power of Indigenous peoples in several different regions of the world						X
	C3.2 analyse the impact of globalization on the political power of Indigenous communities and organizations						X
	C3.3 analyse the exercise and balance of power between parties involved in various contemporary conflicts over the land, culture, and/or livelihood of Indigenous communities						X
C4. The Concept of Self-Determination demonstrate an understanding of the concept of self-determination, exploring a variety of perspectives on and arguments for Indigenous sovereignty/self-governance	**C4.1** explain the evolution of self-determination as a core principle and fundamental right in international law						X
	C4.2 analyse a variety of perspectives on and models of Indigenous sovereignty/self-governance to identify some arguments in support of Indigenous nationhood and self-determination						X
	C4.3 explain various challenges that self-determining Indigenous communities face as settler governments create, ratify, and implement international treaties that affect these communities						X

  ISBN: 978-1-77492-140-1

D. Legal, Political, and Social Action							
D3. Education and Capacity Building demonstrate an understanding of the significance of educational capacity, including capacity for language education, in protecting, preserving, and revitalizing Indigenous cultures	**D3.2** analyse the methods and results of a variety of Indigenous community initiatives to revitalize Indigenous languages and preserve Indigenous knowledge						X
D4. Social Action and Global Leadership demonstrate an understanding of key factors that influence social action, and analyse various initiatives to support Indigenous aspirations and perspectives globally in terms of the leadership strategies they employ	**D4.1** analyse the political and/or national context for a range of social action regarding issues of concern to Indigenous peoples to determine some factors that support or obstruct such action						X
	D4.2 explain some ways in which non-governmental organizations and forums around the world share knowledge and attempt to influence government perceptions of Indigenous realities, evaluating the impact of various strategies and initiatives						X
	D4.3 analyse the approaches of Indigenous leaders to developing community capacity for sustainable self-governance in terms of their use of the two-eyed seeing model						X
	D4.4 analyse the approaches of Indigenous leaders to global environmental protection in terms of their use of the two-eyed seeing model						X

  ISBN: 978-1-77492-140-1

LESSON 1

HOW DO WE READ GRAPHIC NOVELS?

DURATION

Two hours

OVERVIEW

Once students have read the first two volumes of the Surviving the City series, they will be challenged with thinking about and discussing the graphic novel format. Comics are a unique medium through which stories are told using multimodal literacies. One format comics take is the graphic novel. Comics activate multiple literacies including verbal, visual, and media literacies (all of which connect to curriculum). This lesson is designed to introduce teachers and students alike to the unique features of this medium. Throughout the lesson, students will research the different aspects of the comics medium and then create their own one-page comic incorporating these parts.

BACKGROUND

The terms *graphic novel* and *comic book* describe the format of a book, rather than a genre. Graphic novels and comic books can be fiction, nonfiction, biography, fantasy, dystopia, or any genre in between.[1] Graphic novels are an accessible reading resource for all students, and they have been proven to engage even the most reluctant of readers.[2] Graphic novels include visual

1 "What is a Graphic Novel?" Get Graphic, the Buffalo and Erie County Public Library and Partnering Organizations, accessed August 1, 2019, https://www.buffalolib.org/get-graphic/what-graphic-novel.

2 Sarah Knutson, "How Graphic Novels Help Students Develop Critical Skills," Resilient Educator, updated October 23, 2018, https://resilienteducator.com/classroom-resources/graphic-novels-visual-literacy/.

devices that shape the story, such as panels and gutters. Graphic novels also include dialogue, characters' thoughts, narration, and captions. Graphic novels are typically read from left to right and top to bottom.

MATERIALS

- writing utensils
- whiteboard or chart paper
- markers
- pencil crayons
- ACTIVITY SHEET: ALL ABOUT COMICS (1.1) (one copy for each student)
- RUBRIC: ONE-PAGE COMIC (1.2) (two copies for each student)
- ANATOMY OF A PAGE (1.3) (one copy for each student)
- computers/tablets with internet access (optional)
- art paper (one sheet for each student)
- variety of comics and graphic novels
- class sets of *Surviving the City* and *From the Roots Up* (volumes 1 and 2 of the Surviving the City series)

ACTIVATE: WORD WALL

For Less Experienced Learners: Ask students what graphic novels or comics they have read in the past. Make a list of these titles on the whiteboard or a sheet of chart paper. Follow this with a list of the parts of a comic with which students are already familiar (e.g., captions, sound effects, thought balloons).

For More Experienced Leaners: Provide students with a variety of comics and graphic novels. Have students choose a page they really like from one of them, and then have students show and discuss with a partner what they like about it and why. This can lead to activating discussion/thoughts about layouts and comic book elements as well. It will later also help students transition into their peer assessments—being able to speak about aspects of the visual storytelling they liked and how the author's stylistic choices impacted their understanding of the story.

ACQUIRE: ALL ABOUT COMICS

Give each student a copy of the ACTIVITY SHEET: ALL ABOUT COMICS (1.1). Read through the worksheet with the class. As you read the worksheet, have students fill in the missing words. Another option is to have students research and record the missing words as a "scavenger hunt" activity, using online and print sources.

Alternatively, have students create their own template to record the parts of a graphic novel.

Next, have students work (in pairs or groups) to find examples of gutters, panels, thought

  ISBN: 978-1-77492-140-1

balloons, dialogue balloons, sound effect balloons, etc., in *Surviving the City* or *From the Roots Up* and discuss how they work together with the illustrations to tell the story.

Finally, assign students the task to read *We Are the Medicine* before beginning lesson two.

Answer Key for Activity Sheet: All About Comics (1.1):

1. gutters
2. a visual or implied boundary, and the contents within it, that tell a piece of the story
3. the space between the panels; as the reader moves from one panel to the next, they predict and conclude what is happening
4. gutters
5. change
6. description
7. focuses on a character's thoughts and ideas
8. focuses on conversation between characters
9. uses onomatopoeia to convey sound in a story
10. dialogue
11. narration
12. motion
13. moving
14. realistic
15. expressions

APPLY: CREATE YOUR OWN ONE-PAGE COMIC

Explain to students that they will now create their own one-page comic. The topic of the comic page can be an event from their day, for example, their commute to school, or an account of an after-school activity.

Students will mirror the process of how comics are made by creating a rough sketch and then a good sketch. Distribute a copy of ANATOMY OF A PAGE (1.3) to students, which has examples and explanations of the first three stages of comic artwork: thumbnails/roughs, pencils, and inks. Ask students what they notice between the thumbnails, pencils, and inks.

Before they begin, distribute one copy of the RUBRIC: ONE-PAGE COMIC (1.2) to each student and discuss it. Then have students plan out their page. Students should write a brief description of what they plan to draw for each panel. Once they have each of their panels planned (e.g., panel one: wake up in bed, panel two: brush teeth, panel three: eat breakfast, panel four: walk to school), have students write the dialogue, thoughts, and other elements that they want to include. Students should aim to incorporate at least four of the different parts of a graphic novel discussed in the Acquire activity. Once they have their page planned, they can begin creating basic visuals using stick figures or crude sketches to block out how many panels are on the page. Have students use their descriptions to sketch a rough draft of their scene in the panels they have created.

For Less Experienced Learners: Have students use graph paper to help guide their pages.

For More Experienced Learners: Have each student fold a sheet of paper in half and in half again, so they have four panels (boxes) on each side to use for their graphic novel scene.

ASSESS: PEER ASSESSMENT AND ONE-PAGE COMIC RUBRIC

Before students submit their one-page comic, have them engage in a peer editing session, using their copies of the RUBRIC: ONE-PAGE COMIC (1.2). Have students exchange their one-page comic with a partner. Then have students review their partner's page several times, and circle the level of proficiency they would give the student. Make sure students write an explanation for the grade they gave in each category, using the back of the rubric to jot down their comments and suggestions for improvement. Remind students that constructive criticism is not personal and should include both positive comments and comments that suggest in a friendly manner an area needing improvement.

Now that they have gone through the editing process—similar to how real comics are made—have students work on their good copy, also referred to as a "pencil draft" in the comic world. Students will revise their work and create a final draft on a fresh piece of paper before submitting the one-page comic for final grading. The final product should have detailed visuals with colour. Use the RUBRIC: ONE-PAGE COMIC (1.2) to assess students.

Date: ____________________ Name: ____________________

ALL ABOUT COMICS

When reading a graphic novel, it's important to understand the different visual elements that make up the story. Fill in the blanks as instructed below.

Panels and____________(1)

Define the following terms.

Panel: ____

____(2)

Gutter: ____

____(3)

Fill in the blanks below to complete the sentences.

Consider the size and shape of panels. How do they fit together? Do they interrupt or overlap each other? Are there any images without panel borders at all? The spaces in between the panels—the ____________(4)—indicate a ____________(5): in how time is passing, in where you are, or in which character you're looking at or talking to. What do the gutters add to how you understand the story?

TEACHER GUIDE FOR SURVIVING THE CITY VOLUMES 1–3 © 2025 PORTAGE & MAIN PRESS ISBN: 978-1-77492-140-1

Date: ______________________ Name: ______________________

ALL ABOUT COMICS

Define the following terms.

__________(6) and Word Balloons

Thought Balloon: ____

____(7)

Dialogue Balloon: ____

____(8)

Sound Effect Balloon: ____

____(9)

Fill in the blanks below to complete the sentences.

Think about how the __________ (10) appears. Are the words different colours? Written with thicker or thinner lines? How would that sound? How about the silence when no one is speaking? Is there any __________ (11) or description (words in boxes, but not spoken)? How is that important to how the story unfolds?

Sound Effects and __________ (12) Lines

Sounds set the scene, signal something off-scene, and add another layer to each story. Motion lines indicate how characters or objects are __________ (13). What sounds do you see? How are each of the sounds written—does the way it's written reflect what it actually sounds like? What gestures do you see?

Art

Every creator has their own style. Is the art __________ (14)? Cartoony? What can you tell from the __________ (15) on faces? The gestures and movement of characters? The background and its details? If there is colour, how does that change over the course of a page? Each chapter?

TEACHER GUIDE FOR SURVIVING THE CITY VOLUMES 1–3 © 2025 PORTAGE & MAIN PRESS ISBN: 978-1-77492-140-1

Date: ______________________ Name: ______________________

ONE-PAGE COMIC

CATEGORY	Excellent	Good	Developing/Needs Improvement
Story Structure /5	The story is very well-organized. One idea or moment follows another in a logical sequence with clear transitions.	The story is well-organized. One idea or moment may seem out of place. Clear transitions are used.	The story is hard to follow. The transitions are sometimes unclear.
Image Choice /10	Carefully chosen images help the reader understand the action and emotions in the story.	Most of the images help the reader understand the story. One or two are unrelated or confusing.	Comic includes a few images that help the reader understand the story.
Elements /10	Four different parts of a graphic novel discussed in the Acquire activity are effectively used.	Three to four different parts of a graphic novel discussed in the Acquire activity are used.	One to two different parts of a graphic novel discussed in the Acquire activity are used.
Grammar & Spelling Conventions /5	Writer makes no errors in grammar or spelling that distract the reader from the story content.	Writer makes a few errors in grammar or spelling that distract the reader from the story content.	Writer makes many errors in grammar or spelling that distract the reader from the story content.
Effort /5	Final product is completed and pride in one's work, proper time management, and adequate planning is evident.	Final product is short, and more effort could have been put into time management and/or adequate planning.	Final product is incomplete—pride in one's work, proper time management, and/or adequate planning is not evident.

Mark out of 35:

  ISBN: 978-1-77492-140-1

ANATOMY OF A PAGE

THUMBNAILS

At the thumbnails (or roughs) stage, the artist translates the information from the script into visual information. It's meant to be very sketchy or rough. The artist will consider how much space each panel should take on the page and how much room is needed for captions and dialogue. They will also consider the best angle to show the action from and what each character's body language should be for the scene. They will think about what should be in the characters' environments and how the characters, environments, and panels should interact. The artist will also choose the reading flow of the page. On this page, the flow, or reading path, moves counterclockwise from the top centre of the page in a circular motion. Even though these characters are shown together, and are texting each other in this scene, the page layout the artist has created shows that they are all still isolated from one another.

PENCILS

The pencils show what the first good copy of the art will look like. During the pencils stage each character is drawn in full detail and should be easy to distinguish from other characters. The details of the characters' facial expressions or environments become clearer, but the original layout choices from the roughs stage stay the same.

INKS

Finally, in the inks, the artist adds different line thicknesses and areas of shadow to emphasize the characters, environments, page layouts, and mood of the scene. Characters and items in the foreground have much thicker lines than items farther away in the background. These differences in line weight add depth perception to a two-dimensional image so readers understand where the characters are positioned in their environment and how close they are to the reader. The heavy black inks help our eye move in a counterclockwise circle around the page from character to character and panel to panel. The dark shadows around the room at the bottom of the page also suggest that this scene is taking place at night, which emphasizes the somber mood of this scene.

TEACHER GUIDE FOR SURVIVING THE CITY VOLUMES 1–3 © 2025 PORTAGE & MAIN PRESS ISBN: 978-1-77492-140-1

LESSON 2

WHAT IS MY IDENTITY?

DURATION

One to two hours

OVERVIEW

Once students have read the entire Surviving the City series, they will be challenged with thinking about and discussing the multiple layers of their identity. Students will read about Tasha Spillett's identity and experiences as an Afro-Indigenous woman, while exploring the layered identities of the characters in Surviving the City. Finally, students will build on their learning in lesson 1 to create a graphic novel character of themselves, using visual representations to communicate their identity.

BACKGROUND

Key terminology in this lesson includes *intersectionality*, *Two-Spirit*, and *Afro-Indigenous.*

Intersectionality refers to the layered marginalization people may experience when they belong to more than one marginalized group in society. The term is used to describe the experiences of people who are marginalized due to more than one aspect of their identity—for example, being marginalized due to their race and also being marginalized due to their gender, or due to their biracial identity, or due to their race and their socioeconomic status, and so on.

Two-Spirit is a term some Indigenous LGBTQ+ people use to describe their spiritual identity as having both a male and female spirit. The term can also be used to describe gender identity (male, female, third gender) and/or sexual identity (lesbian, gay, bisexual, queer). Many

  ISBN: 978-1-77492-140-1

Indigenous communities and individuals around the continent are working to restore Two-Spirit teachings and roles in community.

The term *Afro-Indigenous* is used to describe people who have both Indigenous and African lineages.

MATERIALS

- "Hair and the Ties That Bind" <https://www.cbc.ca/newsinteractives/features/hair-and-the-ties-that-bind> by Tasha Spillett
- computers/tablets with internet access
- class set of *We Are the Medicine*, volume 3 of the Surviving the City series
- writing utensils
- art paper
- pencil crayons
- RUBRIC: ONE-PAGE COMIC (1.2) (from lesson 1)

ACTIVATE: IDENTITY WORD WALL

Inform students that today's lesson will be about identity. To begin, have students work in pairs or small groups to create or add images and words that are important to their identities on a piece of chart paper, shared online document, or whiteboard space.

Have students explain—to the class, small group, or a partner—why they chose these words and images, and how they relate to their identity.

Debrief the activity by asking the following questions:

- What do you notice about the identities that make up our classroom?
- What types of things do people usually point to when asked about their identity?

ACQUIRE: TWO-SPIRIT DISCUSSION, AFRO-INDIGENOUS DISCUSSION

Ask the class if anyone knows what the term *intersect* means. Solicit student responses.

Prompt their memories by drawing a Venn diagram consisting of two intersecting circles. Ask them to point to the area of the diagram that represents the *intersection*.

Next, ask the class if anyone knows what the term *intersectionality* means.

For Less Experienced Learners: Inform students that different layers of our identities can affect us in different ways. If someone is good at basketball but struggles in art, they may be treated with respect and admiration on the court, but not treated like that in the art room. This example of a layered identity highlights how various aspects of our identities can influence the ways people treat us in different spaces. Intersectionality, on the other hand, refers to aspects of people's identities that historically and presently lead to them being treated unequally in society, or *marginalized*. The term marginalization thus refers to the hurtful and unequal ways some people are treated based on their identities (such as race). And intersectionality refers to the experience of having two different marginalized identities.

For More Experienced Learners: Inform students that intersectionality refers to "the layered marginalization people may experience when they belong to more than one marginalized group in society."[3] For example, people experience layered oppression due to a combination of their race and gender, or biracial identity, or race and socioeconomic status, and so on, in cases where both of these identities are marginalized.

For All Learners: Read "Hair and the Ties That Bind" by Tasha Spillett at <https://www.cbc.ca/newsinteractives/features/hair-and-the-ties-that-bind> with the class. This is a personal essay about her identity and experiences as an Afro-Indigenous woman.

Have students work in small groups to discuss the following questions:

- How does Tasha say she navigates her identity as an Afro-Indigenous woman?
- Which characters in the Surviving the City series face marginalization due to more than one aspect of their identities?
- How do the characters around them empower or disempower them?
- What are some of the layered aspects of your own identity?

APPLY: IDENTITY COMMUNICATION

Have students choose one character from *We Are the Medicine*. Ask them to verbally describe and explain to a partner how their visual representations—posture, clothing, hairstyle, accessories—communicate their identity.

Next, inform students that they are going to use their knowledge about the parts of a graphic novel from lesson 1 to create themselves as a cartoon character. Have students write a brief description of how they plan to draw themselves. Have them think about clothing, accessories, and hairstyles. Students could also consider what kind of art style might represent their personality. Students should aim to incorporate at least four of the different parts of the graphic novel introduced in lesson 1. Students will need to explain the visual elements they've included to communicate their identity, using speech bubbles, thought bubbles, or captions. Help guide their work by asking: "What can we understand about using symbols, colours, or stereotypical visual elements in our design choices?"

Once they have their character planned, have students use their descriptions to sketch a rough draft of their character.

---

3 "Intersectionality," *Anti-Oppression*, Simmons University Library, accessed March 9, 2024, https://simmons.libguides.com/anti-oppression.

ASSESS: CO-CONSTRUCT CRITERIA AND SELF-ASSESSMENT RUBRIC

As a class, compare the RUBRIC: ONE-PAGE COMIC (1.2) from lesson 1 to this new task, and work together to adjust the rubric as you see fit. For example, the class may decide to change the number of graphic novel elements that are required, or even create a new rubric category.

Before students submit their character designs, have them engage in a peer editing session, using the revised rubric. Have students exchange their character designs with a partner. Then have students review their partner's design several times, and circle the level of proficiency they would give the student. Make sure students write an explanation for the grade they gave in each category, using the back of the rubric to jot down their comments and suggestions for improvement. Remind students that constructive criticism is not personal and should include both positive comments and comments that suggest in a friendly manner an area needing improvement.

Now that they have gone through the editing process—similar to how real comics are made—have students work on their good copy. Have students revise their work and create a final draft on a fresh piece of paper before submitting their character design for final grading. The final product should have detailed visuals with colour. Use the revised rubric to assess students.

If available, give students the option to create their final copy using digital tools.

  ISBN: 978-1-77492-140-1

LESSON 3

WHAT DOES IT MEAN TO BE AN ALLY?

DURATION

One hour

OVERVIEW

Throughout this lesson students will learn about allyship, including definitions, actions, and discussions about which characters in the Surviving the City series act as allies. Finally, students will have the opportunity to create ally statements in solidarity with marginalized groups.

BACKGROUND

Allyship can be defined as "a proactive, ongoing, and incredibly difficult practice of unlearning and re-evaluating, in which a person of privilege works in solidarity and partnership with a marginalized group of people to help take down the systems that challenge that group's basic rights, equal access, and ability to thrive in our society."[4]

MATERIALS

- RUBRIC: ALLYSHIP STATEMENT (3.1)
- computers/tablets with internet access
- projection device
- class sets of the Surviving the City series

4 Lila Watson and others, "If you have come," *Black Lives Matter*, California State Polytechnic University Pomona, accessed March 9, 2024, https://libguides.library.cpp.edu/c.php?g=1047593&p=7681898.

  ISBN: 978-1-77492-140-1

ACTIVATE: ALLYSHIP CONCEPT MAP

Begin by asking the class if anyone knows what an *ally* is. Solicit students' responses and begin making a concept map on the board.

Next, read this quote to the class:

> "If you have come to help me, you are wasting your time. But if you have come because your liberation is bound up with mine, then let us work together."

Inform students that this popular quote was crafted by a group of Aboriginal rights activists from Queensland, Australia, in the 1970s. They are speaking to potential allies. Ask the class:

- What do you think *liberation* means in this quote?
- What new understandings of allyship do you have from hearing this quote?
- What are some actions that people can do to show allyship?

For All Learners: Ask students to think about a time when they were thankful someone stood up for them or helped them feel more comfortable in a space. What did the person do that made them feel more welcome or comfortable? How can we make sure others feel welcome and comfortable in our spaces?

For More Experienced Learners: Inform students of the ALLY acronym from Kayla Reed, an African American woman and Executive Director of Action, a grassroots racial justice organization working to build power for Black people in the United States.

A – always center the impacted

L – listen and learn from those who live in the oppression

L – leverage your privilege

Y – yield the floor[5]

After sharing the acronym with students, ask:

- What new actions and understandings of allyship do you have from Kayla Reed's acronym?

---

5 Kayla Reed (@iKaylaReed), "A-always center the impacted," Twitter (now X), June 13, 2016, https://x.com/iKaylaReed/status/742243143030972416.

ACQUIRE: DISCUSSION OF ALLYSHIP IN THE SURVIVING THE CITY SERIES

Either as a whole class, or in small groups, have students discuss the following:

- Which characters in the Surviving the City series would you describe as allies?
- Describe the actions that those characters took that make them an ally.
- Has anyone in your own life acted as an ally? If so, how?
- Have you ever acted as an ally towards a group? If so, how?

APPLY: ALLYSHIP STATEMENTS

For Less Experienced Learners: Inform the class that they will now have the opportunity to create an allyship statement, in solidarity with new students to the school. Ask: "How can we ensure new students feel welcome in the classroom? In the school?"

For More Experienced Learners: Inform the class that they will now have the opportunity to create an allyship statement in solidarity with one or more marginalized groups. It is up to you whether to facilitate students creating an allyship statement towards a group discussed in Surviving the City such as Indigenous peoples, Two-Spirit peoples, Afro-Indigenous peoples, or another marginalized group of your choosing.

To begin, project the four Calls to Action addressed to "All Our Relations," found on pages 28 and 29 of *The Findings of C2C: Two Spirit & Queer/Trans People of Colour,* a Call to Conversation hosted by the University of Winnipeg in 2019, in partnership with Two-Spirited People of Manitoba Inc. and Queer & Trans People of Colour (QTPOC): <https://www.uwinnipeg.ca/c2c/docs/c2c_calls-to-action_final.pdf>. Also draw students' attention to the "Calls to Action—Community," "Calls to Action—Education," "Calls to Action—Government," and "Calls to Action—Arts and Culture" found elsewhere in this booklet, as they may wish to reference these while working on their allyship statements.

Based on this framework for allyship towards Two-Spirit people, challenge the class to think about how these Calls to Action could apply to acting as allies to other groups.

Using the ideas in this booklet, plus the ideas students generated through the concept map and class discussions, have students, either as a whole class, in small groups, or individually, create an allyship statement about how they will act as allies towards a marginalized group.

ASSESS: CO-CONSTRUCT CRITERIA FOR STATEMENTS

For Less Experienced Learners: Before beginning to create the allyship statement for new students, co-construct the criteria for the whole-class allyship statement. First, review Algonquin Anishinaabe Dr. Lynn Gehl's "Ally Bill of Responsibilities" at <http://www.lynngehl.com/uploads/5/0/0/4/5004954/ally_bill_of_responsibilities_poster.pdf>.

  ISBN: 978-1-77492-140-1

For More Experienced Learners: Once students have gotten started, but before they finish their statements, bring the class together to co-construct the criteria for the allyship statement. Project or display the RUBRIC: ALLYSHIP STATEMENT (3.1)

For All Learners: Project or display the RUBRIC: ALLYSHIP STATEMENT (3.1) and ask the following questions:

- What should be included in the allyship statement?
- How long should the allyship statement be?
- What format should the allyship statement be in? (Paragraph form, point form, visual representation, etc.)
- What makes an excellent allyship statement? What makes a good allyship statement, and what makes an allyship statement need improvement?

Based on student ideas, fill in the RUBRIC: ALLYSHIP STATEMENT (3.1).

  ISBN: 978-1-77492-140-1

Date: ____________________ Name: ____________________

ALLYSHIP STATEMENT

CATEGORY	Excellent	Good	Developing/Needs Improvement

  ISBN: 978-1-77492-140-1

3.1

LESSON 4

WHY IS CULTURE IMPORTANT?

DURATION

One to two hours

OVERVIEW

Throughout this lesson, students will learn about various aspects of Anishinaabe culture—including the Berry Fast mentioned in *Surviving the City*; smudging, Powwow dancing and drumming, and Two-Spirit teachings in *From the Roots Up*; and sharing circles and tobacco offerings in *We Are the Medicine.* Students will then have an opportunity to research and share something from their own cultures.

BACKGROUND

Culture is an important aspect of identity formation. Culture includes many seen and unseen aspects of a group or society, including clothing, food, language, folklore/stories, literature, gender roles, humour, approaches to medicine and health, rules of conduct, pride, concepts of justice, notions of modesty, and attitudes towards the environment.

MATERIALS

- projector for presentations
- access to computers/tablets with slideshow software
- RUBRIC: ORAL PRESENTATION (4.1) (two copies for each student)
- RUBRIC: ORAL PRESENTATION (4.2) (one copy for each student)
- class sets of the Surviving the City series

ACTIVATE: THINK/PAIR/SHARE

Have students turn to a partner and discuss how they would define the word *culture*. Have a student volunteer look the definition up in the dictionary and inform the class.

As a class, create your own definition. Solicit responses from the pairs and, as a class, co-construct a definition of culture that includes language, traditions, social norms, art, and values. Write this definition on the board for students to refer back to throughout the lesson.

Next, ask students to turn to their partners again and name things that reflect culture (e.g., clothing, food, language, stories, celebrations).

Solicit oral responses from the pairs.

Discuss with students that *culture* is a complex term that includes many seen and unseen parts. Some things that we can see include clothing, jewellery, food, language, folklore/stories, literature, holidays, and festivals.

Some unseen parts include family roles, beliefs and assumptions, self-concepts, relation to authority, core values, biases, body language, manners, beauty ideals, attitudes towards school, family values, gender roles, humour, approaches to medicine and health, rules of conduct, pride, concepts of justice, notions of modesty, attitudes towards the environment, competitiveness, expectations, child-rearing practices, gestures, and even personal space.

Ask the class if anyone knows what *cultural appropriation* is. Solicit responses from the groups. Have a student volunteer look the definition up in the dictionary and inform the class. Ask students if they can give some examples of cultural appropriation. Examples might include non-Indigenous clothing designers copying traditional Indigenous designs for their clothing and selling it for a profit. Next, explain that Canadian copyright law protects Indigenous knowledge, including traditional cultural expressions.[6] This means that it is illegal to profit off of the culture of Indigenous Peoples in Canada. However, there are some grey areas—for example, some oral stories may be difficult to protect. Discuss with students that it is generally considered wrong to profit off of a culture that is not your own.

For Less Experienced Learners: Ask the class to consider the following questions:

- Are the books of the Surviving the City series considered authentic Indigenous texts? Why? (Yes, because the author identifies as Nehiyaw and Trinidadian and is writing from an Indigenous perspective. Authentic texts present authentic Indigenous voices, depict themes and issues important to Indigenous Peoples, and include respectful portrayals or representations of Indigenous Peoples and their traditions and beliefs.)

---

6 Innovation, Science and Economic Development Canada, "Indigenous Peoples and Intellectual Property," accessed October 1, 2019, https://ised-isde.canada.ca/site/intellectual-property-strategy/en/indigenous-peoples-and-intellectual-property.

  ISBN: 978-1-77492-140-1

- Which cultures are represented in the Surviving the City series? (Miikwan is Anishinaabe, Dez and Riel are Ininew, Ginebeg is Afro-Indigenous.)
- What are some of the similarities and differences between your own culture and the ones represented in the series?
- Who belongs to multiple cultures in the series? (Ginebeg is Afro-Indigenous.)
- Reconciliation is the repairing of relationships. What can the Surviving the City series teach us about reconciliation? (There is still a long way to go before reconciliation will be achieved. The series highlights ways Indigenous Peoples heal their communities by loving each other, attending ceremonies, and fighting for their rights.)

For More Experienced Learners: Ask the class to consider the following questions:

- Are the books in the Surviving the City series considered authentic Indigenous texts? Why? (Yes, because the author identifies as Nehiyaw and Trinidadian and is writing from an Indigenous perspective. Authentic texts present authentic Indigenous voices, depict themes and issues important to Indigenous Peoples, and include respectful portrayals or representations of Indigenous Peoples and their traditions and beliefs.)
- What are some of the themes in the Surviving the City series? (Indigenous topics such as the effects of genocide and intergenerational trauma, the harmful legacy of the residential school system including the unmarked graves of children, Missing and Murdered Indigenous Women and Girls and Two-Spirit people, the importance of ceremony in fostering resilience, and the importance of friendship and family.)
- What can the Surviving the City series teach us about how cultures change or evolve over time? (See the discussion about changing protocols around who can sit at the drum in *From the Roots Up*, p. 41.)
- In what ways does the Surviving the City series teach us how aspects of our identities intersect? Which characters have multiple layers to their identities? (For example, Ginebeg belongs to African culture, Indigenous culture, Canadian culture, and maybe even the specific culture of his home community.)
- What are some of the ways your own identities intersect? (For example, some groups with physical impairments, like those who are Deaf, belong to a proud Deaf culture, separate from their ethnic and national backgrounds; the school students attend has a school culture; people belong to online groups which subscribe to gaming cultures; and so on.)
- Reconciliation is the repairing of relationships, including the recognition that Indigenous Peoples are equal members of society. What can the Surviving the City series teach us about reconciliation? (There is still a long way to go before reconciliation will be achieved. The series highlights ways Indigenous Peoples heal their communities by loving each other, attending ceremonies, and fighting for their rights.)

ISBN: 978-1-77492-140-1

Next, explain to students that they are going to explore the significance of culture for Indigenous Peoples and for themselves.

ACQUIRE: ORAL STORYTELLING

Have students help you invite an Elder or Knowledge Keeper to speak to students about a local Indigenous cultural activity. See Inviting an Elder Into Your Learning Space on page 8 for guidelines around inviting an Elder or Knowledge Keeper to your class.

Depending on the time allotment, the next section might fit into a different class. Ensure students have a chance to talk and debrief with the Elder or discuss their thoughts on the article before the end of the first class.

In addition (or as an alternative), have students read one of the following articles:

- "My Berry Fast" by Akeesha Footman from *Muskrat Magazine*: <https://muskratmagazine.com/my-berry-fast/>. The Berry Fast ceremony featured in *Surviving the City* is part of Anishinaabe (also known as Ojibwe) culture.
- "Anishinabek circles a traditional yet new way to smooth out the 'injustices of the system'" by Erik White (CBC News): <https://www.cbc.ca/news/canada/sudbury/circles-program-anishinabek-nation-1.7035978>
- "My Drum is Two-Spirit" by Sâkihitowin Awâsis from *Red Rising Magazine*: <https://www.redrising.ca/post/my-drum-is-two-spirit-sâkihitowin-awâsis>

For Less Experienced Learners: Choose one of the articles to read to the class.

For More Experienced Learners: Organize students into small groups. Distribute one article to each group. Have each group read, discuss, and summarize the article together. Debrief the activity as a class and have a representative from each group share what they learned from their article with the whole class.

To review, conduct a class discussion and ask the following questions to ensure comprehension and understanding:

- What is the purpose of the cultural activity you learned about?
- Why is it important?
- What life lessons does it help teach?
- How is the cultural activity presented in the Surviving the City series? (if applicable)
- Why do you think the author included it in the Surviving the City series? (if applicable)

APPLY: MY CULTURE ORAL PRESENTATION ASSIGNMENT

Explain to students that they will now have the opportunity to reflect on and teach the class about something important from their culture. Distribute one copy of the RUBRIC:

ORAL PRESENTATION (4.1) to each student. Explain that their oral presentations must be accompanied by a slide show and should answer the following questions:

- Describe the cultural activity.
- What is the history of this activity?
- How is this activity honoured or recognized in the present day?
- What important lessons does this activity teach?
- What is your personal experience with this activity?

Allow students time to reflect on an aspect of their culture that they would like to share. Have students interview family members and conduct research to find answers to their questions.

Students' presentations should be about 3–5 minutes long. Encourage students to show pictures throughout.

ASSESS: PEER EDITING AND PRESENTATION RUBRIC

Distribute a copy of either the complete RUBRIC: ORAL PRESENTATION (4.1) or the blank RUBRIC: ORAL PRESENTATION (4.2). For the blank rubric, either as a whole class or in small groups, have students read through the project description and discuss what important criteria should be included in each category. Fill in the characteristics of presentations that are developing (needs improvement), good, and excellent.

Before students present, have them engage in a peer-editing session. Have students pair up and practise their presentations with their partner. Have the listening student circle the level of proficiency they would give the presenter. Make sure students write an explanation for the grade they gave in each category, using the back of the rubric to jot down their comments and suggestions for improvement. Remind students that constructive criticism is not personal and should include both positive comments and comments that suggest in a friendly manner an area needing improvement.

Once students have finished practising their presentations, allow them time to make revisions before their final presentations are due.

Grade students' presentations using the RUBRIC: ORAL PRESENTATION (4.1 or 4.2).

Date: ______________________ Name: ______________________

ORAL PRESENTATION

CATEGORY	Excellent	Good	Developing/Needs Improvement
Knowledge and Understanding /20	The presenter displays an in-depth knowledge about the cultural activity, its historical context, and its significance.	The presenter displays a decent amount of knowledge about the cultural activity, but may be missing information about historical context or significance.	The presenter displays a limited knowledge about the cultural activity and its historical context and significance.
Visual Appeal /5	The presentation is highly appealing to the audience. Pictures and other multimedia formats are utilized throughout.	The presentation is somewhat appealing to the audience.	The presentation is not appealing to the audience.
Grammar & Spelling Conventions /5	Writer makes no errors in grammar or spelling that distract the reader from the content in the multimedia presentation.	Writer makes one or two errors in grammar or spelling that distract the reader from the content in the multimedia presentation.	Writer makes three or more errors in grammar or spelling that distract the reader from the content in the multi-media presentation.
Presentation Skills /5	The presenter maintains eye contact and appropriate tone/voice throughout the presentation.	The presenter maintains some eye contact and appropriate tone/voice throughout the presentation.	The presenter does not make eye contact and/or does not have appropriate tone/voice throughout the presentation.

Total out of 35 marks:

Date: ______________________ Name: ______________________

ORAL PRESENTATION

CATEGORY	Excellent	Good	Developing/Needs Improvement
Knowledge and Understanding /20			
Visual Appeal /5			
Grammar & Spelling Conventions /5			
Presentation Skills /5			

Total out of 35 marks:

  ISBN: 978-1-77492-140-1

LESSON 5

WHAT IS WELLNESS FROM A HOLISTIC PERSPECTIVE?

DURATION

One hour

OVERVIEW

> **NOTE:** For this lesson, have students help you invite an Elder to speak to the class about their Nation's teachings or perspectives of wellness, such as teachings about the Medicine Wheel or Sacred Hoop and its significance in some Indigenous cultures, including Anishinaabe culture. See Inviting an Elder Into Your Learning Space on page 8 for suggestions about inviting Elders to speak to students.
>
> Consider adapting this lesson based on the perspectives of the Elder.
>
> Remember that Medicine Wheel teachings and other cultural practices should only be shared with students by an Elder or Knowledge Keeper.

Schools often don't explicitly teach students how to be *well*. Throughout this lesson, students will learn about holistic perspectives of wellness. Many Indigenous Nations think of wellness as relating to all parts of the self: physical, mental, emotional, and spiritual. Students will set goals in each of these categories to facilitate holism, balance, and wellness in their lives. Students will learn the value of self-care, and why it is especially important while learning about difficult topics, such as those presented in the Surviving the City series.

  ISBN: 978-1-77492-140-1

MATERIALS

- whiteboard
- writing utensils
- scrap paper
- writing paper

ACTIVATE: SELF-CARE WHOLE-CLASS DISCUSSION

Inform the class that today's lesson will be centred on the concept of wellness. Wellness as defined from an Indigenous (and more specifically, Anishinaabe) perspective is when all the parts of ourselves—physical, spiritual, mental, and emotional—are in balance.

Begin the discussion by asking:

- What does it mean to be *well?*

Write students' answers on the whiteboard, so students have a visual as to what wellness might look and feel like. Inform students that wellness looks and feels different to different people, and that it is important for us to know what wellness looks and feels like for us personally.

ACQUIRE: WELLNESS LESSON

Explain to students that they will think about the four parts of the self—physical, mental, spiritual, and emotional—and how it is important for the parts to be balanced if we truly want to be well. Advise students that we are also doing this activity to ensure that we can look after ourselves while learning about difficult topics, such as those presented in the Surviving the City series.

Provide students with information regarding the mental health supports that are available to them in the school and community. If possible, bring in a school counsellor to teach students about mental health and healthy coping skills. Create a list of healthy coping skills as a class, so students can choose the skills they are most likely to use to set goals.

Have students set goals for themselves that fit each part of the self and write the goals on scrap paper. Explain that some goals may fit with two or more parts, but that they should pick the one that makes the most sense for them. It may be helpful to give some examples of goals for each category:

- Physical goals (health, fitness): I will lift weights once per week.
- Spiritual goals (religious, focusing on self, family, community or anything that makes our "spirit" happy): I will practise my culture with my family once a month.
- Mental goals (knowledge, school): I want to learn about outer space.
- Emotional goals (mental health): I will practise deep breathing when I feel stressed.

Students should set at least three goals for each of the four categories.

ISBN: 978-1-77492-140-1

APPLY: SMART GOALS

For Less Experienced Learners: Instruct students to write goals in a positive format: instead of saying "I will eat less sugary foods," they can make the statement positive by writing not what they will do less of, but what they will do more of. For example, "I will eat more vegetables." Allow students the option to talk with a partner to share goal ideas, or make a list of goal ideas together as a class. Once there are a lot of ideas for students to use as a springboard, give students time to update their goals.

For More Experienced Learners: Once students have at least three goals relating to each part of the self, have them transform their goals into SMART goals. SMART stands for Specific, Measurable, Attainable, Realistic, and Time-bound. Give students an example such as the following:

- Physical goal: I will eat healthy.

Notice how this goal is not in the SMART goal format, as it is not specific, measurable, or time-bound. This goal should be changed to incorporate these elements:

- I will eat three servings of vegetables every day.

OR

- I will limit myself to one sugary snack a day.

Have students revise their goals as needed and record a final draft of their SMART goals on a fresh piece of paper.

ASSESS: GOAL ASSESSMENT

For Less Experienced Learners: Since this assignment is highly personal, it is often difficult to grade. An option is to have students read out three of their goals to you, so you can assess if the goals begin with "I will" and are written as positive statements.

For More Experienced Learners: Since this assignment is highly personal, it is often difficult to grade. An option is to have students read out three of their goals to you, so you can assess if the goals are SMART goals:

- Specific
- Measurable
- Achievable
- Realistic
- Time-bound

ISBN: 978-1-77492-140-1

An example of a SMART goal is as follows:

- I will weight train once per week.

It is specific (instead of saying something vague like "I want to be stronger"); it is measurable, meaning you can easily identify if you accomplished the goal or not; it is achievable and realistic (you're not saying you are going to win a weight-lifting competition anytime soon, unless you are close to doing that already!); and it is time-bound, meaning you will do this every day, week, month, or year.

EXTENSION: CHECK-IN ACTIVITY

Have students self-assess their progress in achieving their goals periodically throughout the year. This could involve asking students which goals they have been working on and which ones they need to improve on. Have students rate how they feel about their goals on a scale of 1–10 and write a short reflection on their progress, including successes and areas they still need to work on.

Meet one-on-one with each student to discuss their wellness levels, and have a conversation about how they can increase their wellness in areas that they rate lower. For example, if a student gives their physical wellness a low rating, have a discussion about why that is and what they can do to improve their wellness for tomorrow (if a student often feels tired, they may want to work on going to bed earlier).

  ISBN: 978-1-77492-140-1

LESSON 6

HOW CAN I CONTRIBUTE TO MEANINGFUL CHANGE?

DURATION

Up to ten hours, including:

- Lesson: one hour
- Idea Jam: one hour
- Introduce project: one hour
- Planning time: two hours
- Preparation time: two hours
- Implementation: one hour
- Attending two other initiatives: two hours

OVERVIEW

Through this project, students will explore resistance in relation to the resurgence of Indigenous identity, culture, language, and land rights by engaging in actions that either educate/raise awareness, advocate for change, support, or lead/inspire/change/create. First, students will explore worldwide resistance movements generally, and then focus in on the issue of Missing and Murdered Indigenous Women and Girls and Two-Spirit People: an issue that is deserving of attention and action. Students will have the opportunity to identify a social cause in their school, classroom, or community that they would like to make a difference towards. They will be responsible for planning and implementing a social-justice action project (a project that works to advance a social cause), as well as attending and reflecting on other groups' action

  ISBN: 978-1-77492-140-1

projects. The goal is that students will contribute to thoughtful, cooperative, and responsible social action, leading to active citizenship and engagement within their communities. This lesson and project can take anywhere from one to two months to complete, depending on the amount of class time students have to work on it.

MATERIALS

- chart paper
- markers
- computers/tablets with internet access
- BOOKLET: SOCIAL-JUSTICE ACTION PROJECT (6.1) (one copy for each student)

ACTIVATE: WORD SPLASH WORLDWIDE SOCIAL-JUSTICE ACTION INITIATIVES

Begin by posing the following questions to students, and soliciting responses:

- What is social justice? (fairness for all people; rooted in human rights and equality)
- Why is social justice work important? (it gets people involved in thinking about solutions to problems in their communities and brings communities together in a positive way)
- What is social action? (taking steps to change the things that are wrong in our society and introducing new ideas and processes for doing things better in the future)
- Do you think the Surviving the City series is a social-justice action initiative? Why or why not? (it raises awareness, provides resources, and protests injustices peacefully)
- Is there an example of social-justice action in the Surviving the City series? What is it? (the Missing and Murdered Indigenous Women and Girls and Two-Spirit People march in *Surviving the City*; the inclusion of Two-Spirit dancers at the Powwow in *From the Roots Up*; the Powwow to honour the children who didn't make it home from residential schools and the Medicine Garden in *We Are the Medicine*)

ACQUIRE: INDIGENOUS RESISTANCE LESSON

Organize students into groups of three or four. Explain that they are going to conduct research and present to the class on an Indigenous Resistance Movement of their choice. Co-construct criteria for this short presentation with the class, such as:

- two to three minutes in length
- must include the 5 Ws (who, what, when, where, why)
- must include at least three pictures

Have each group select an Indigenous Resistance Movement from across the continent, country, or their local territories. Some examples might include the following:

- Idle No More <http://www.idlenomore.ca/>
- Standing Rock <https://americanindian.si.edu/nk360/plains-treaties/dapl.cshtml>
- Bear Clan Patrol <https://bearclanpatrol.org>
- Missing and Murdered Indigenous Women and Girls and Two-Spirit People <https://www.rcaanc-cirnac.gc.ca/eng/1448633299414/1534526479029> and <https://www.cbc.ca/news/politics/mmiwg-inquiry-deliver-final-report-justice-reforms-1.5158223>
- Barriere Lake Solidarity <https://web.resist.ca/~barrierelakesolidarity/>
- Klabona Keepers <https://warriorpublications.wordpress.com/tag/klabona-keepers/>
- Oshkimaadziig Unity Camp <https://ammsa.com/publications/windspeaker/camp-used-reconnect-people-traditional-agreements>
- Unist'ot'en Camp <https://unistoten.camp>
- The Yinka Dene Alliance <https://www.ammsa.com/publications/windspeaker/yinka-dene-alliance-group-british-columbia-first-nations>

APPLY: IDEA JAM CAROUSEL ACTIVITY

For Less Experienced Learners: Give students a list of social-justice action projects that they are likely to have heard about before. Examples might include Orange Shirt Day, Red Shirt Day, and perhaps the Green Team initiative at your school (if applicable). Ask students to describe how each fits into the category of a social-justice action project.

For More Experienced Learners: Organize students into four groups. In their groups, have students read the recommendations in the report from the National Inquiry into Missing and Murdered Indigenous Women and Girls[7] and discuss ideas for their upcoming social-justice action projects.

For All Learners: Distribute a sheet of chart paper and markers to each group. Assign each group a different action station to brainstorm around: Educate/Raise Awareness, Advocate for Change, Support, or Lead/Inspire/Change/Create. The following are some examples of ideas they might discuss:

7 National Inquiry into Missing and Murdered Indigenous Women and Girls, *Reclaiming Power and Place: The Final Report of the National Inquiry into Missing and Murdered Indigenous Women and Girls* (2019), https://www.mmiwg-ffada.ca/final-report/.

1. Educate/Raise Awareness
    - conduct research
    - prepare and deliver a class speech about an important issue
    - create a social media campaign
    - hand out pamphlets to educate others about an issue
2. Advocate for Change
    - write a letter to a Member of Parliament or to the school principal
    - arrange a meeting to discuss an issue with a local politician
    - start a school-wide petition
3. Support
    - fundraise for a local charity
    - attend and help out at a community event
    - volunteer at a local organization
4. Lead/Inspire/Change/Create
    - start a school lunch group dedicated to your issue
    - create a social media campaign
    - create a memorial or medicine garden at your school

Give groups five minutes to discuss and write down all the possible ideas for their social-justice action projects they can think of in that category before they switch to the next station. As groups go from one station to the next, they are challenged to come up with new ideas that haven't been written down yet.

Once students have had a chance to brainstorm at each station, have them review the possibilities for their own social-justice action projects. What activity would they like to do for their project?

Assign students a grade out of five based on their engagement in the group brainstorming activity.

APPLY: PLANNING YOUR ACTION PROJECT

For Less Experienced Learners: Hand out a copy of the BOOKLET: SOCIAL-JUSTICE ACTION PROJECT (6.1) to each student. Explain that as a class, they will be working together to identify an issue they are passionate about, create a plan to address the issue in their classroom, school, or larger community, and then implement the plan.

Review the booklet with students, as well as the due dates for each section. Model filling out the booklet together as a class. Have students volunteer for roles in the action project such as:

  ISBN: 978-1-77492-140-1

- Planners: This group comes up with the plan, which includes a scheduled event, and is responsible for ensuring the plan is on track. They will meet with each group and help solve problems as they arise.
- Artists: This group is responsible for coming up with the advertising material (if applicable), information sheets (if applicable), and/or creating the resources such as the brochures or posters (if applicable).
- Connectors: This group is responsible for using their connections to get people involved as participants in the project. Need an audience? This group will help bring them.
- Do-ers: This group is responsible for doing anything else that needs to be done! Need someone to hang signs? This group will do that.

For More Experienced Learners: Hand out a copy of the BOOKLET: SOCIAL-JUSTICE ACTION PROJECT (6.1) to each student. Explain that they will be working in groups of three to five to identify an issue they are passionate about, create a plan to address the issue in their classroom, school, or larger community, and then implement the plan.

Review the booklet with students, as well as the due dates for each section. Have students plan and implement their own social-justice action project in their group. Ensure students have adequate class time to plan and implement their project, and meet with students regularly to ensure that their projects are on track and feasible. Once students have their project date, time, and location planned, create a sign-up sheet for students to sign up to attend at least two other action projects.

APPLY: IMPLEMENTING YOUR ACTION PROJECT

Meet with each group periodically throughout the process to ensure that groups' plans are realistic and respectful. Make sure to attend all the social-justice action project initiatives' scheduled events in order to effectively grade the assignment.

ASSESS: ACTION PROJECT SCORE GUIDE

Use the Action Project Score Guide to assess students' research and reflections throughout the project.

Name: ______________________________

SOCIAL-JUSTICE ACTION PROJECT

WHAT IS A SOCIAL-JUSTICE ACTION PROJECT?

An action project involves working cooperatively with classmates to address a problem you see in your class, school, or wider community. You will be working in groups of three to five to identify a social cause or problem, plan a community action project, and implement the project in your classroom, school, or wider community.

WHAT IS THE GOAL OF IMPLEMENTING A SOCIAL-JUSTICE ACTION PROJECT?

The goal is to contribute to thoughtful, cooperative, and responsible social action, leading to active citizenship and engagement with your communities.

PROJECT OVERVIEW

Step 1: Whole Class Idea Jam (5%)

What is your group's mission? How can you accomplish your mission?

Mission Examples

- Raise awareness about hunger in your city/town
- Create a safe space for 2SLGBTQ+ students
- Combat cyber bullying by creating a positive social media campaign

Step 2: Plan (30%)

Choose a mission and the best way your group can accomplish its mission and develop a proposal, which includes a scheduled event.

Step 3: Implement (50%)

Implement the plan! Actually create something or do something that positively affects the school and/or community and brings people together.

Step 4: Reflect (5%)

Did your project work? What made it successful? What could have been done differently?

Step 5: Attend and Reflect on Other Initiatives (10%)

(only applicable to classes that did not do a whole-class project)

Did you attend and reflect on at least two other initiatives?

ISBN: 978-1-77492-140-1

STEP 2: PLAN

Choose an issue and develop a plan to address/solve the issue.

Issue:____

Explain the significance of your issue. Why does this issue matter? Who/what is affected by the issue? Why did you choose this particular issue?

ISBN: 978-1-77492-140-1

Organizations that are already addressing this issue (list in bullet form):

 ISBN: 978-1-77492-140-1

What is your solution to your issue/problem? What are your action project goals/objectives?

How are you going to ensure that people hear about your initiative? How will you ensure your plan will succeed?

  ISBN: 978-1-77492-140-1

Resources/Supplies Needed (list in bullet form):

Who will do what? Assign roles.

  ISBN: 978-1-77492-140-1

Possible Problems and Concerns (as well as how they will be addressed):

Timeline:

  ISBN: 978-1-77492-140-1

STEP 4: REFLECT

Did your project work? What made it successful? What could have been done differently?

TEACHER GUIDE FOR SURVIVING THE CITY CITY VOLUMES 1–3 ISBN: 978-1-77492-140-1

STEP 5: ATTEND AND REFLECT ON OTHER INITIATIVES

Action Project Attended:

Date:

Response:____

Action Project Attended:

Date:

Response:____

ISBN: 978-1-77492-140-1

ACTION PROJECT SCORE GUIDE

1. IDEA JAM (5%)

i. Educate/Raise Awareness
ii. Advocate for Change
iii. Support
iv. Lead/Inspire/Change/Create

2. PLAN (30%)

i. Explain the significance of your issue.
ii. Why does this issue matter?
iii. Who/what is affected by the issue?
iv. Why did you choose this particular issue?
v. Organizations that are already addressing this issue
vi. What is your solution to your issue/problem?
What are your action project goals/objectives?
vii. How are you going to ensure that people hear about your initiative?
How will you ensure your plan will succeed?
viii. Assign Roles
ix. Possible Problems and Concerns
x. Timeline

3. IMPLEMENT (50%)

i. Did you attend and participate fully in your own implementation event?
ii. Did you ensure the event was successful?
iii. Did you attend to any issues that may have arisen?
iv. Did you leave a lasting impression on people?

4. REFLECT (5%)

i. How did your event go?
ii. What would you do differently next time?

5. ATTEND AND REFLECT ON OTHER INITIATIVES (10%)

i. Did you attend at least two other initiatives and reflect thoughtfully on them?

  ISBN: 978-1-77492-140-1